FEMEN

FEMEN

BY

FEMEN

With Galia Ackerman

Translated by Andrew Brown

polity

First published in French as *FEMEN* © Éditions Calmann-Lévy, 2013

This English edition © Polity Press, 2014

Polity Press
65 Bridge Street
Cambridge CB2 1UR, UK

Polity Press
350 Main Street
Malden, MA 02148, USA

ISBN-13: 978-0-7456-8321-8
ISBN-13: 978-0-7456-8322-5(pb)

A catalogue record for this book is available from the British Library.

Typeset in 10.75 on 14 pt Janson Text by
Servis Filmsetting Ltd, Stockport, Cheshire, SK2 5AJ
Printed and bound in Great Britain by Clays Ltd, St Ives plc

The publisher has used its best endeavours to ensure that the URLs for external websites referred to in this book are correct and active at the time of going to press. However, the publisher has no responsibility for the websites and can make no guarantee that a site will remain live or that the content is or will remain appropriate.

Every effort has been made to trace all copyright holders, but if any have been inadvertently overlooked the publisher will be pleased to include any necessary credits in any subsequent reprint or edition.

For further information on Polity, visit our website: www.politybooks.com

CONTENTS

 MANIFESTO

IN THE BEGINNING WAS THE BODY, THE
SENSATION THE WOMAN HAS OF HER OWN
BODY, THE JOY OF ITS LIGHTNESS AND
FREEDOM. THEN CAME INJUSTICE, SO HARSH
THAT IT IS FELT WITH THE BODY; INJUSTICE
DEPRIVES THE BODY OF ITS MOBILITY,
PARALYSES ITS MOVEMENTS, AND SOON YOU
ARE HOSTAGE TO THAT INJUSTICE. THEN YOU
PUSH YOUR BODY INTO BATTLE AGAINST
INJUSTICE, MOBILIZING EACH CELL FOR THE
WAR AGAINST THE WORLD OF PATRIARCHY
AND HUMILIATION. YOU SAY TO THE WORLD:

OUR GOD IS WOMAN!
OUR MISSION IS PROTEST!
OUR WEAPONS ARE BARE BREASTS!
HERE FEMEN IS BORN, AND HERE BEGINS
SEXTREMISM.

FEMEN

Femen is an international movement of bold, topless activists whose bodies are covered with slogans and whose heads are crowned with flowers.

The activists of Femen are women who are specially trained, physically and psychologically, ready to perform humanist tasks of every degree of complexity and provocation. The activists of Femen are ready to face repression, and their motivation is exclusively ideological. Femen: the crack troops of feminism, its fighting vanguard, a modern incarnation of the Amazons, fearless and free.

OUR IDEOLOGY

We live in a world under the economic, cultural and ideological occupation of men. In this world, woman is a slave deprived of any right to ownership and, in particular, any right of ownership over her own body. All the functions of the female body are subjected to strict control and regulation by patriarchy.

A woman's body has become separated from her, becoming the object of monstrous patriarchal exploitation. Total control over the female body is the main instrument of woman's oppression. Conversely, a female sexual tactic is the key to her liberation. Woman's proclamation of her rights over her own body is the first and most important step towards her liberation. Female nudity, liberated from the patriarchal system, undermines that system. It is the manifesto of struggle and the sacred symbol of female liberation.

Femen's naked-bodied attacks lie at the heart of the historical conflict between 'woman' and 'the system', and they are its most obvious and appropriate illustration. The naked body of an activist expresses unconcealed hatred for the patriarchal order and the new aesthetic of the feminine revolution.

OUR OBJECTIVE

Total victory over patriarchy.

OUR MISSIONS

- By the power of daring and personal example, to pass a comprehensive feminine sentence on patriarchy as a form of slavery.
- To provoke patriarchy into open conflict by forcing it to demonstrate its anti-human, aggressive essence so as to discredit it once and for all in the eyes of history.
- To ideologically undermine the fundamental institutions of patriarchy, dictatorship, the sex industry, and the Church, by submitting these institutions to diversionary tactics such as trolling, to obtain their complete moral capitulation.
- To make propaganda for the new revolutionary feminine sexuality, as opposed to patriarchal eroticism and pornography.
- To inject modern women with the culture of an active resistance to evil and the fight for justice.
- To create the community that is most influential and best able to fight in the world.

OUR DEMANDS

- The immediate political reversal of all dictatorial regimes that create intolerable living conditions for women; in the first place, the rule of theocratic Islamic states practising *sharia* and other forms of sadism vis-à-vis women.

- The total eradication of prostitution, the most brutal form of women's exploitation, by criminalizing the clients, investors and organizers of this slave trade. The absolute and universal separation of Church and state, with a ban on any interference on the part of religious institutions in the civil, sexual and reproductive lives of modern women.

OUR TACTICS: SEXTREMISM

Sextremism is the main new form of feminist activism developed by Femen.

Sextremism is female sexuality that has risen up against patriarchy by embodying itself in extreme political acts of direct action. The sexist style of these actions* is a way of destroying the patriarchal idea of the predestination of female sexuality, in favour of its great revolutionary mission. The extreme nature of sextremism is a manifestation of the superiority of Femen activists over the vicious dogs of patriarchy. The form of unauthorized sextremist actions expresses woman's historical right to protest in any place and at any time, without coordinating her actions with the patriarchal structures that maintain order.

Sextremism is a non-violent but highly aggressive form of activism; it is a super-powerful, demoralizing weapon that undermines the foundations of a corrupt patriarchal culture.

---

* The French word 'action' is here used both in the sense of a 'direct action' and a 'demonstration' of an artistic-political kind. It has links with what in the English-speaking world are (or were) often known as 'happenings' or 'performance art', and – as the Femen themselves point out – with the politico-aesthetic movement known as 'actionism'. (Trans. note.)

OUR SYMBOLS

The crown of flowers is a symbol of femininity and proud disobedience. It is the crown of heroism.

The body-as-poster is a truth expressed by the body with the help of nudity and the signs drawn upon it.

The Femen logo is the Cyrillic letter Φ (F), which mimics the shape of the female breasts, the main symbol of the women's movement Femen.

Femen's motto: my body is my weapon!

OUR STRUCTURE AND ACTIVITY

The international movement Femen carries out activities on the territory of democratic countries and reserves the right to act on the territories controlled by dictatorial regimes. Femen is registered as an international organization, and is currently establishing national Femen groups throughout the world. It seeks to expand the geography of its activity by attracting new activists. The preparation of sextremists is carried out in several training centres such as in France. The movement is led by a coordinating council which includes the founding members of the movement and its most experienced activists.

OUR FINANCING

To ensure the activities of our organization, Femen accepts donations from people who share its ideas and methods of combat. Femen also sells clothing and accessories with its symbols, and art objects of its own making. The movement is not dependent on any investor and refuses on principle to accept any financial assistance from political parties, religious organizations, or other lobbyists.

All the funds earned and collected serve the goals of the movement.

The only source of distribution of Femen's production is the site: <http://www.femenshop.com>.

INFORMATION

Femen professes the principle of openness to the media, to ensure maximum media coverage of its revolutionary activity in defence of women's rights.

At the same time, the movement is involved in a campaign for information and aggressive propaganda on the Internet, using the Web to transmit its ideology. Femen is present on all major social networks and communities on the Net.

The official sources of information on the activities of the Femen movement are the website <http://www.femenshop. com> and the Facebook page <http://www.facebook.com/ Femen.ua>.

Femen, Kiev, January 2013

A MOVEMENT OF FREE WOMEN

Preface by Galia Ackerman

At the age of fourteen or fifteen, these girls started to get bored. Their friends spent their time drinking beer out in the street and chatting or taking drugs, but none of these four young Ukrainian girls were really into any of this. In their poor backwoods towns, Anna Hutsol, Inna Shevchenko, Oksana Shachko and Sasha Shevchenko were looking for a meaning to their lives. With the help of a few Soviet books, they fantasized about the days when communist youth built up the country. That was before their time. Only Anna, a little older than the other three, could remember her early Soviet days, a happy childhood which for her has the taste of tangerines and chocolate.

Although they had heard of Stalin's crimes, as far as they were concerned this was all in the distant past, while in the last years of the USSR, their parents lived peaceful lives and felt useful and respectable. Of course, reality was more complex and much less rosy, and concealed profound inequalities. But for them, nothing could be compared to the toxic atmosphere of the 1990s or the 2000s. The girls felt hatred for the wild west-style capitalism that allowed a happy few to get rich quickly and scandalously, and that laid waste the lives of ordinary people, including their families.

Against this backdrop of a loathing for capitalism in its post-Soviet guise, Sasha, Oksana and Anna discovered a circle of Marxist-influenced people holding street discussions in their hometown, Khmelnytskyi, in western Ukraine. A group of young people met regularly to study Soviet philosophy textbooks found in attics, as well as the works of Marx, Engels and the nineteenth-century German socialist August Bebel.

These young people were opposed to the current political and moral consensus.

During perestroika and in the early post-Soviet years, it was customary – in Russia as in Ukraine – to denigrate the Soviet period.

In Ukraine, national grievances had been superimposed on this discourse: the Soviet regime was accused of political and cultural imperialism, as well as crimes against the Ukrainian nation. President Yushchenko demanded that the UN recognize the artificial famine of 1932–3, which killed nearly 6 million people in Ukraine, as genocide.

And so, if we stick to the economy, both in Russia and Ukraine, official propaganda presented this liberalism – a liberalism that amounted to the plundering of national wealth by a handful of oligarchs close to the government – in the same way as did the Harvard School: it was seen as the only viable alternative to the dark communist past. In reality, this interpretation mainly gave a fake legitimacy to grossly unequal regimes. The power of the propaganda machine was such that, apart from the communist parties – viewed as backward-looking vestiges from the past – voices advocating social justice were very rare.

In this atmosphere of liberal diktat, it required a certain intellectual audacity to claim kinship with Marxism in the same way as other radical factions, such as the current Left Front of Sergei Udaltsov in Russia. The street circle of Khmelnytskyi continued to evolve, and some of its members, including three of the future Femen, tried putting into practice the lessons learned, by founding an association for student aid.

Meanwhile, for an entire year, the girls studied Bebel's *Women and Socialism*, which became their favourite book. It was a real revelation and they decided to dedicate themselves to fighting for the freedom of women. In Bebel, they found a 'scientific basis' for their spontaneous hatred of misogyny and capitalism, as well as of the religion that oppresses women, always and everywhere. Armed with this reading, Anna, Sasha and Oksana excluded their male friends from the association and created a new movement, New Ethics. Soon they moved to Kiev.

From spring 2008, their actions, which had initially been innocent and childish, involved dressing up and making a splash. They pondered. What should they protest against? How to find targets? During one of their brainstorming sessions, they found their first big topic: Ukraine is not a brothel. They rebelled against the sex industry that flourished in the country, under the aegis of the government, and against Westerners' perceptions of Ukrainian women, those 'Natashas' ready to fall into the arms of a 'Prince Charming' for a pittance or the promise of a *dolce vita* abroad.

During this struggle, which involved dozens of actions, the movement became more structured and renamed itself 'Femen'. In 2009, Inna, a student in Kiev who came from another provincial city, Kherson, joined the trio from Khmelnytskyi. These four were the backbone of the group. Gradually, Femen found its trademark: a young topless woman with a crown of flowers on her head. In this book, they explain in detail the meaning of this 'outfit' that makes them recognizable worldwide.

In 2009, power in Ukraine was still in the hands of the coalition that emerged after the Orange Revolution. This revolution was a disappointment for many Ukrainians because the government – partly hampered by the global crisis – turned out to be unable to improve the economic situation in the country and to fight corruption. At the end of 2009, the country was polarized on the eve of the presidential election. Viktor Yanukovych, defeated in 2005, faced both the outgoing president Viktor Yushchenko and Yulia Tymoshenko, the former muse of the revolution who in the meantime had become an opponent and rival to Yushchenko. As in the past, Yanukovych was supported by the Russian regime.

The Femen, who do not want to be limited to issues traditionally seen as 'feminine', decided to join in the political struggle. They took up a position that would give them a very negative press in the eyes of many Ukrainians, choosing to be neither for the 'blue' camp of Yanukovych, whom they considered as a puppet of the big oligarchic capitalists of east Ukraine, nor for the 'orange' camp (supporters of Yushchenko or Tymoshenko), because of their political and economic fiasco. They harboured a particular hatred for Tymoshenko, an elegant and charismatic woman who was prime minister from December 2007 to March 2010, because in their view she did nothing to combat the sex industry or to improve the status of women. However, once Yanukovych had assumed power, the situation soon became clear to the girls. Despite its flaws, the Orange Revolution had brought several freedoms, while the regime that took over was becoming increasingly repressive. From this period, Femen grew politically more radicalized. Their new enemy was dictatorship. The police, the judiciary and the SBU, the security service of Ukraine (an offspring of the Soviet KGB), kept them under surveillance. They experienced their first appearances in court, their first stays in jail and their first interrogations by SBU officials.

They realized that fighting for women's rights in today's Ukraine would be difficult and would involve rebelling against the police state. They also realized that Ukraine would never be free while Russia was governed by the 'Putin system', and they saw themselves as morally obliged to support the Russian opposition as it challenged the massive frauds perpetrated in the general elections of 2011. Femen undertook a series of spectacular actions both against the Yanukovych regime, in Kiev, and the Putin regime, in Moscow: they were held in Russian prisons.

What is extraordinary in Femen, and makes them very special in the post-Soviet arena, is their openness to the outside world. These girls respond to the status of women or the drift towards dictatorship in Ukraine, but they also show their solidarity with the democratic struggle of others. After their protests against the Putin regime – protests that were not actually much to the liking of the Russian opposition movement, which is too inward-looking and unappreciative of the boldness of these 'little Ukrainian girls' – they decided to attack the regime of Alexander Lukashenko, the Belarusian president who is considered to be the last dictator in Europe. Their Belarusian tour in December 2011, where they fell into an ambush laid by the sinister local KGB, was probably their most terrible experience. It could have ended in real tragedy. In two or three years, the girls had become seasoned fighters who, with their naked bodies covered with caustic slogans, were defying police officers armed with batons.

Quickly, they embarked on a new battle. As atheists since

their teens, they have fully assimilated Marx's famous phrase, 'religion is the opium of the people'. For them, religion is a tool for patriarchy to dominate women. The Femen therefore decided to launch an attack on clericalism, whether Islamic or Christian, because it is always women who suffer from it. After protesting in 2010 against the Iranian judicial decision to stone Sakineh Mohammadi Ashtiani to death, they gave a major role to anti-clerical struggle in their actions, from 2011 onwards. They were protesting in the Vatican and Kiev, in Moscow and Istanbul, in Paris and London.

We need to understand how much the Femen are going against the grain in Russia and Ukraine. In these countries, the Orthodox Church, which was persecuted in the Soviet period, has risen from the ashes but is gradually placing itself at the service of the state, to the point where it has become the de facto state religion in Russia. The Femen denounce its reactionary and outdated teachings, and its collusion with corrupt regimes. They denounce it even more violently than do the women of Pussy Riot. With the same energy and determination, they address the medieval practices of countries where *sharia* law prevails. They are not afraid of brushing against the spirit of tolerance of our Western societies: they call a spade a spade. In their view, for example, Europe must refuse to accept the wearing of the niqab or burqa. 'Muslim woman, get undressed!' – this is the slogan that best summarizes the appeal made by Femen to the Muslim women of the world, and especially those who live in the Western world.

Thanks to their anti-clericalism, the ideology of Femen can take on sharper edges. They are carrying out spectacular and more dangerous actions against what they see as the three manifestations of patriarchy: the sex industry, dictatorship and clericalism. Added to this are, of course, their purely anti-capitalist demands such as their actions at the

World Economic Forum in Davos. According to Femen, women are the first victims of the poverty imposed by the masters of the world.

The European media, but also the media of many other countries, eagerly cover the actions of Femen. It's as much the form as the content that attracts them. Each time, they can watch a mini-drama where the spectator's interest is aroused by the danger faced by the women taking part. Reports on Femen rarely explain their doctrine, but abound in spectacular photos. And of course, these young women are the food and drink of directors of documentaries.

How could it be otherwise? These girls sound the alarm on the bell tower of the cathedral of Kiev, climb the walls of the enclosure at Davos under the noses of snipers positioned on the roof, protest topless outside the largest mosque in Istanbul and attack the Catholic fundamentalists of Civitas disguised as 'naughty' nuns, wearing the inscription 'In Gay We Trust' on their chests. And snapshots of them fighting with the cops or security services are all part of the 'show'. We are confronted with a new phenomenon: the Femen use the means of an increasingly radical artistic actionism for purely political reasons, while deliberately refusing to recognize themselves as artists. This is the price these bold women pay, in full awareness, for the dissemination of their ideas.

In autumn 2012, the Femen moved to France, while maintaining their office in Kiev. It was at this time that I made their acquaintance. I met Inna, then the other three founders, Oksana, Sasha and Anna, passing through Paris. I built up this book from dozens and dozens of hours of interviews with them. These are their words. Why did I want to write this book for them?

As a journalist and expert on Russia and the post-Soviet

world, I had for several years been interested in the phenomenon of young radicals who preach Marxism and socialism, despite the disaster represented by the Soviet experience. The way I imagined Femen – as young idealist girls rebelling against untamed capitalism in its oligarchic version – was largely confirmed upon my first contact with them.

But I discovered much more than this: four young women of extraordinary courage, creative and modern and, above all, full of compassion for the women in distress around the world. And because they feel a genuine compassion, they are also capable of a fierce hatred for those who cause suffering. In this, they are of the same metal as the great revolutionaries. The Femen seem to me to be the heirs of the long line of rebellious women from the Tsarist era, such as Vera Zasulich, Vera Figner, Catherine Breshkovsky, Alexandra Kollontai, and many others. But of course, in the age of the Internet and of show business, their passion can lead to very different results. Instead of drifting into terrorism, the Femen, radical at heart, have found a method of tackling their enemies that is both fun and highly symbolic: they use the naked body instead of a gun or a bomb.

So why did I decide to help them tell their stories? Despite a number of ideological differences (I'm not a Marxist and I'm agnostic rather than atheist), I feel close to their struggle. I can only share their revolt against the sex industry, which is an abomination. But it is especially their fight against dictatorship that inspires me with the greatest sympathy. In Soviet times, I systematically supported dissidents and, nowadays, the democrats who oppose Putin's regime and other autocratic regimes in the post-Soviet world. I was and remain a close friend of some key figures of dissent and opposition in Russian politics, such as Anna Politkovskaya, Elena Bonner, Alexander Ginzburg, Vladimir Bukovsky and Sergei

Kovalev, just to name a few, even if some are unfortunately no longer among the living. And I maintain my friendship with a great Ukrainian dissident who lives in France, Leonid Plyushch.

That leaves their anti-clericalism. The Femen are convinced atheists who believe that all religion oppresses women. This is historically true, but different religions have not evolved in the same way. Protestants and liberal Jews have come a long way in giving women an equal place to men. The Catholic Church, once the Church of the Crusades and the bonfires of the Inquisition, is also changing slowly but surely. However, the Russian Orthodox Church, faithful to its Byzantine and Tsarist traditions, has become the pillar of the Putin regime. This government, which for years has crushed political opposition and the free press, and which finally lost its legitimacy in the last general election marred by massive fraud, relies more than ever on the Church which, for its part, is taking this opportunity to extend its influence, including in Ukraine. Should we tolerate this collusion between the Putin government and the patriarchal Church, some of whose hierarchs have emerged from the KGB? For me, the answer is no. Without sharing their militant atheism or supporting some of their actions, their denunciation of the positions of the Orthodox Church seems justified.

Far beyond their glamorous political activities, the adventures of these four young Ukrainian women are well worth being known and understood.

These ardent girls, who advocate resolutely European values, are a symbol of hope for our old continent, even if we do not always agree with their ideas or methods. It is as if it were from an all too often disregarded Eastern Europe that the vanguard of bright, bold forces were disembarking. What will the future of Femen be? Their Paris training centre, open to activists from around the world, is there to train the 'soldiers' of feminism, so as to attack the oppressors of women and to allow women to be free and fulfilled. Is this the beginning of a global feminist revolution, something for which Femen yearn? We can only hope so.

Part I

THE GANG OF FOUR

We're sometimes called the 'gang of four'. 'We' are Inna Shevchenko, Sasha Shevchenko (it's a very common name in Ukraine, we're not related), Oksana Shachko and Anna Hutsol. And ever since we formed the core of Femen, we've been inseparable. Three of us, Anna, Oksana and Sasha, are from the same town in western Ukraine, Khmelnytskyi. There we started to study philosophy and to be politically active, before arriving in Kiev. As for Inna, she comes from the town of Kherson, near Odessa, and she joined the other three founding members of Femen in Kiev, to become the fourth 'pillar'.

What was life like for each of us before Femen? In what families did we grow up? Why did we feel the need to fight for women's rights? How did we become atheists in a post-communist Ukraine where religion is taking over in ever more important areas?

1

INNA, A QUIET HOOLIGAN

I was born in a 'godforsaken hole' in southern Ukraine, in other words in a small provincial town, Kherson. They speak Russian there, like in Odessa, which isn't very far away. It's still a very Soviet town, where the USSR still seems to be in existence and nothing ever changes. It was in this quiet town, that's infuriated me ever since my childhood, that I very soon started to tell myself I'd make a life for myself elsewhere.

When I was a little girl my only friends were boys, and I loved climbing trees. I dressed in shorts and sneakers; I hated dresses. This made Mom furious: she really didn't like the fact I wasn't like a model little girl. I didn't even refuse to wear dresses, but Mom just knew I'd immediately get them dirty and tear them, either by climbing an oak tree or playing with stones on a construction site. Near our apartment block, there was one such site and in the evening, when the workers left, our little gang invaded it and built castles out of the bricks. I needed freedom, and instead of playing with dolls or messing about in a sandbox, I preferred to join the boys on more out-of-the-way expeditions. I didn't want to be a boy, but I liked having them round me. I was a kind of quiet hooligan, who never took part in fights. The only person I quarrelled with from time to time was my older sister.

Apart from that, I was a well-behaved child. My parents never gave me a spanking. In fact, I'm lucky to have a very nice family. I'd define my mother as an 'ideal woman' for Ukraine. She was a chef in a restaurant before becoming chef in a university cafeteria. She's a typical Ukrainian woman who works full time but also keeps her house spotless, cooks, and takes care of her husband and children without losing her temper or, more precisely, without ever showing her emotions – a nice, quiet, positive and very pleasant woman. But she's not a fulfilled woman, even if she doesn't complain about anything. She bears her fate, like a donkey carries its load, without realizing she could have had a different life. I suffered for her. In those days, I didn't know the word 'feminism', but I thought this life was unfair. And the fact it was the norm was no consolation to me. I realized early on that I never would live like her. On the other hand, my sister, who's five years older than me, completely internalized this model. In fact, she married at nineteen, had a child at twenty-one, and lives and works in Kherson. However, we've remained very close, and she's always supported me.

Dad is a very emotional man, sometimes short-tempered, but he has a good heart too. In the family, we never had any real arguments. With his sense of humour, my father's always turned any conflict into a mere joke. Our parents argued with my sister and me, without it ever turning nasty.

Dad's a retired soldier, a former major in the troops of the Ministry of the Interior. I'll never be able to imagine him without his uniform. During our childhood, when our parents went out, my sister and I would take turns to dress up in Dad's uniform, but we never had any desire to try on Mom's dresses or high heels. And when he got promoted, we'd make a hole in his epaulette to screw in a new star. For us, it was a sacred ritual!

If I got good grades in school and worked hard, this was also thanks to my father. He always talked to me as if I was a grown-up and kept telling me I was studying for myself, for my future. When I started at primary school, he told me that my adult life was about to begin. I quickly realized that there was a hierarchy at school: some children are better liked by the teachers, who straightaway help them and stimulate them. It's a virtuous circle: if you work hard, you're appreciated by the teachers, and they push you to develop your abilities and become even better. From the first year, I wanted to be the class representative. And I conducted the first electoral campaign of my life. I was elected by a show of hands. In fact, the role gave me a serious responsibility because it meant keeping a register of late arrivals and absences, organizing and lining up the pupils for outings and so on. I held this position throughout my time at school, up until my final exams.

Around the age of twelve, I went through a bit of a crisis. I suddenly realized that the boys preferred girls with dresses and pretty little shoes. As I wanted to be first in everything, I started to dress in a more feminine way and I grew my hair down to my waist. The effect was instantaneous: a lot of boys fell in love with me, including some of my friends. There were plenty of girls who wanted to be my friend because I was the leader of the class, but I thought they were airheaded chatterboxes and I kept my distance. I'd just one girlfriend who was also an excellent pupil. We shared the same table and with her I felt comfortable. In my class, out of twenty-two pupils, there were only seven boys. With my one girlfriend and these boys, we formed a separate group, away from the other girls.

When I was about fourteen, I developed a new ambition: I got it into my head that I'd become president of the school. For us, this was an important function, much more than being just class representative. The school president attends school board meetings and voices the wishes and grievances of the pupils. He or she also organizes competitions and festivals – an important personage, in short. And then the title itself is rather flashy: president! In theory, you can take on this post when you're in the fifth year of secondary school but, in general, pupils vote for people who are in their final year. So my chances of being elected in the fifth year were almost zero. Still, I decided to stand against the nine other candidates. We campaigned for three weeks. We handed out leaflets and each made two public presentations of our platforms. These presentations took place in the main hall where candidates had to go on stage and try to convince the audience. Almost all the pupils took part in the elections, we all wanted to play at democracy, that game for adults. In each class there were ballot papers and boxes. The count was conducted by teachers and pupils drawn by lot.

The day after the election, our class was on duty to maintain order in the school. As class representative, I had specific obligations: I had to place pupils at monitoring stations in the canteen, the schoolyard and so on. Just then, the headmistress ran up and whispered in my ear that I'd won. It turned out that I'd won the majority of votes in thirteen classes out of fifteen – it was an outright victory! That was how my career as president started, and I was re-elected twice, in the last two years at school. This was my first 'political' experience, an unforgettable one, the start of which coincided with the 2004 presidential campaign.

The two main presidential candidates in Ukraine were

Viktor Yushchenko and Viktor Yanukovych, who was backed by the outgoing President, Leonid Kuchma. Back in Kherson, everyone supported Yanukovych, both my family at home and the teachers at school. And then pressure was put on us too. For example, Mom told us that, at her workplace, officials in the local government had threatened to fire anyone who voted for Yushchenko. I tried to explain to my mother that this was bollocks, but she was scared. In eastern Ukraine, most people were aware that Yanukovych wasn't a good candidate, but, out of fear of retaliation or indifference, many were ready to vote for him in spite of everything.

I remember propagandists from the Donbas, the stronghold of Yanukovych, claiming, 'He's a local lad, he went to prison, like so many other people, for snatching hats.'[1] This kind of activity is usually carried out by small-time thugs who snatch the hats off people's heads and only give them back if they're given a few coins in exchange. That said, metaphorically speaking, this is how the majority of Ukrainians live – committing petty crimes to survive when they're living in poverty. So it was a clever propaganda technique to present Yanukovych as a man of the people challenging the intellectual Yushchenko, the candidate of the Ukrainian-speaking elite and married to an American. The Yushchenko couple also spoke Ukrainian at home, and their children wore traditional costumes, shirts with embroidered collars, which was both incredible and intolerable for people in eastern and southern Ukraine. Indeed, the Soviet propaganda that supported Yanukovych presented Ukrainian nationalism as a kind of backwardness. To have a career, you absolutely had to be Russian-speaking.

At the same time, people wanted change, and all Yanukovych could offer was a continuation of the crooked Kuchma regime. A new man, a new background, a new face, but the same words, whereas the 'extra-terrestrial'

Yushchenko had something really original and interesting to say. He called on Ukraine to foster links with Europe and the West and to escape from the Russian yoke, and his appeals carried home. Then there was the story about Yushchenko being poisoned with dioxin during the campaign – we still don't know who was behind it: it led to a wave of sympathy for him. The election campaign was very eventful. Even though I was too young to vote, I understood that Yanukovych could represent neither the interests of the country nor mine. For me, this former petty criminal who 'snatched hats' and couldn't even express himself correctly in his native language, Russian, let alone Ukrainian, was shameful. As president of the school, I attended the educational committee meeting at which the headmistress, who liked me and thought highly of me, openly called on the teachers to vote for Yanukovych. I didn't have the right to protest at the meeting, but the next day I launched into my act. I braided my hair and arranged the braid around my head to look like Tymoshenko, Yushchenko's main ally. I turned up at school with my hair like that, with an orange ribbon tied to my briefcase. Seeing me, my main teacher took me outside and forced me to undo my braid. She confiscated my orange ribbon and told me school wasn't a place for politics. I then asked why the headmistress was openly getting involved in politics, but the teacher, who was actually very fond of me, just asked me to keep quiet. I was really shocked.

I was even more gutted when the official results of the election were announced: Yanukovych was declared the winner. This announcement provoked a revolt in Kiev and also in the provinces, known as the 'Orange Revolution'. This was an idealistic period in the history of independent Ukraine. It was also at this time that I learned about political activism. Everyone was talking about democracy, on television and in the streets. It was a new buzzword, especially in my region. Hundreds of thousands of protesters stood fast in the cold weather of December 2004. They camped for nearly two months out on the central square in Kiev, known as the Maidan. Even in the little, apolitical towns such as Kherson, people who had never been interested in politics took part in fights between 'Orange' supporters and the 'Blues' who were on the side of Yanukovych. That was the most important thing: for a few months, people ceased to be indifferent. Too bad this revolution turned sour later, despite Yushchenko's victory, achieved in the third round under pressure from protesters.

After these few tumultuous months, I returned to my studies. The general level of education was awful but we still learned English better than the average students in Ukraine. By now, my hopes were pinned on winning the gold medal at the end of my studies. I badly wanted a medal, but it didn't work out that way. To win a medal in the provinces, where the quota was very limited, you needed to get high marks not only in your last year at school, as in Kiev, but also in the two previous years. Unfortunately, I'd got one 'good', instead of a 'very good' mark a couple of years back, and that was enough to put me out of the running. I couldn't stop crying!

Despite not winning this medal, which would have helped me gain admission to college, I decided to try for a place on the journalism course at the best university in the country, the National University of Kiev, named after the great Ukrainian poet Taras Shevchenko. Mom tried to change my mind by suggesting I should stay in Kherson, where there's also a university. To her way of thinking, it was absurd to want to go to Kiev when my home and my parents were in Kherson. I couldn't understand her logic: how could she not want the best for her child?

I left for Kiev with Dad. I took seven exams in a month. The day after each examination, at 7 a.m., I ran into college to look at the lists and see whether I'd been eliminated or not. It was a really horrible few days . . . Finally, I won a place in spite of the competition – there were five of us after each place – but I had to pay. In Ukraine, there are very few free places for higher education, and in practice they're reserved for children of MPs and politicians. For an ordinary person, it's simply impossible to benefit from free education, even if you're a genius from a very poor family.

The first day in college, I felt like . . . a little girl from the provinces. Almost all the other students came from Kiev, from wealthy families. They'd already toured round half of the planet, while I was still just discovering the capital city of my own country. I was ashamed to show how little I knew of what they were talking about. I was so aghast that I even wondered if coming to this prestigious location hadn't been a terrible mistake. However, I immediately started thinking up ways to impose my leadership because I couldn't see myself otherwise than as a leader. It wasn't easy, but one month later I was elected head of my study group, and in the same year I was elected president of the parliament of university students.

At Shevchenko University, they elect a parliament composed of students from all faculties, then this parliament elects its own president. So my role was to represent the students vis-à-vis the rector and the professors, to convey their demands and to inform the staff of students' problems. For me, this was an excellent school for political struggle. The young people in the students' parliament are often the children of real deputies – the younger generation intent on going into politics. There were some really interesting people among them, and several of these became friends of mine.

That said, my daily life wasn't easy. I lived in the students' residence, which was a long way from the main building of the university. The parliament sessions took place every Wednesday between 8 p.m. and 11 p.m., and I went home around 1 a.m., which was very difficult in winter when it's dark and the temperature drops well below zero. Mom kept moaning on the phone: 'What's the point of it all?'

I was alone in Kiev, without any family. Yet I started to love this great, bustling city and I didn't suffer from loneliness. In my second year, I was contacted by the city administration. One of them had seen me in the student parliament and was favourably impressed. During the interview at the city hall, they told me: 'You're a promising journalist, come and work with us.' I was thrilled – it was a prestigious job, a real dream for a budding journalist like me.

So I started working for the press service of the Kiev city hall, and my first thrilled response quickly evaporated. In fact, I cried every night, realizing that I'd over-romanticized the world of journalism. Each morning they assigned me my task for the day: I'd have to churn out a report on the mayor or one of his assistants who'd solved a particular difficulty, to the great satisfaction of his fellow citizens. The problem was that I knew full well these were lies, but I had to comply. My reports appeared in various Kiev newspapers, with different bylines. The newspapers were paid by the city administration for all these publications, of course.

All this happened in 2009, while Yushchenko was president. That's why I say the Orange Revolution quickly turned sour. In actual fact, the ruling elites, and especially the big capitalists behind them, never changed. It was the same people, those who'd taken the reins of power when Ukraine became independent in 1991, who still retained control of the country. They simply changed their look: now they wear Brioni suits instead of raspberry-coloured jackets, like the Mafia at the start of the post-Soviet era. But they're essentially the same: they still have the same way of thinking and the same dishonesty, and in addition they're stupid. Their strength is that they gang up and support each other. Even in his supposedly democratic entourage, Yushchenko was a rare bird, an idealist. At least I hope so, because I still have illusions about him. He's a man of integrity who managed to leave power in 2010 while still preserving his dignity, but he wasn't a good politician and failed to reform the system.

In fact, I now realize that even when I was still a child, I was looking for a purpose. At school and in my first year at college, I dreamed of becoming a politician and sitting in a real parliament, not in a school or student parliament. My life changed when I met the trio of Femen: Anna, Oksana and Sasha. It was winter, late 2008 or early 2009. I corresponded with Sasha Shevchenko on Facebook, with no particular aim in mind, just: 'Hi! Your name's Shevchenko? So's mine.' We arranged to meet up in McDonald's, and she suggested I should meet 'the girls', without giving further details. They used to get together in the Ban'ka cafe,[2] located in a Turkish bath dating from the Soviet era. It was a rather dirty place, with typically Soviet tiles. I felt like I was back in Kherson. At the cafe, there was a long table and thirty or so girls sitting round it. They were planning an action against prostitution. That's where I heard the name 'Femen' for the first time. At first I was all at sea. I didn't really warm to them to start with – I didn't know what feminism was all about. I had the weird idea that feminists were women with shaved heads, who wanted to look like men and wore men's clothing. In short, ugly women who didn't get laid enough. But right from the start, I liked their energy – the readiness for action that I'd always been looking for.

2

ANNA, THE INSTIGATOR

My family is Ukrainian. As my name, Hutsol, indicates, my father is of Hutsul origin. This small ethnic group of mountain-dwellers live in the Carpathians and speak a specific dialect of Ukrainian: they've been immortalized in *Shadows of Forgotten Ancestors*, the film by Sergei Parajanov. However, my father's family preserved nothing of this legacy – they moved to the Khmelnytskyi region, in western Ukraine, a long time ago. My parents met at a wedding, but shortly afterwards my father had to go to the Murmansk region in the far north to make a living. My mother, who barely knew him, decided to join him. Just like that, on a whim. They got married and brought me into the world, in 1984. Then my sister followed. My father was a trucker in a mine. I loved looking at the snapshot where he is pictured next to his wagon. He seemed so small compared to the wheel of the truck! I thought he was an extraordinary man, simply because he could handle such a huge machine. I was in awe of him. When the Soviet Union broke up in late 1991, my parents returned to Ukraine.

They're now divorced. From time to time, Mom would tell me: 'Your father is an idiot!' So I asked her why she married him. She replied: 'At twenty, I had to get married, and anyway, he was a good dancer.' Rather a strange reason! They married just like that and had two children, without really loving one another. For me, family is an important concept, and I wouldn't like to tell my children that their father's an idiot. Fortunately, Mom finally understood my arguments, and stopped insisting I get married as soon as possible.

My Soviet childhood was happy. I remember hazelnut ice cream, fresh tomato juice, tangerines, chocolate and snow. Returning to independent Ukraine was more difficult. The kolkhozes – the agricultural cooperatives – were dying out, and to give a bit of support to agriculture, the state handed out abandoned houses to young families. My parents had a house in a village, quite well equipped with running water and a real toilet, which was almost a luxury at the time. But the rest left a lot to be desired. In the 1990s, there was no work and no pay, so my parents dedicated themselves to their kitchen garden. How awful, all those hours spent planting and pulling out potatoes! I was obsessed by just one idea: to work hard at school to get into college, no matter where. The main thing was to escape from the village!

It was mostly the attitude of the villagers towards women that encouraged me to leave as soon as possible. The women toiled like convicts, looking after the fields, vegetables, livestock, laundry, meals, children and housework, while the men just drank. Every house had its own still, and they went round to each other's houses to enjoy a drink together. When they'd drunk their fill, they kicked up a shenanigans and started beating their wives. Each drunkard was master in his own home. My father, disorientated by the loss of his job as a trucker and the enforced idleness that followed, adopted this lifestyle. My mother, sister and I did all the work but he mistreated us and claimed he was the boss. At fourteen, I told my mother to get a divorce. Mom didn't want to; she said that we needed a father. I took my things and left for my grandmother's place, in an even more remote village. I walked to school; it was 7 kilometres away. Meanwhile, my father continued to drink and beat my mother. She eventually divorced him.

My father went to Moscow and found a job as a worker in a porcelain factory, in Lobnya. It was a very physical job, and hard work: he stopped drinking. He'd never have managed to keep going otherwise. He remarried and my mother did the same. She gave me our house as a present, and a plot of 10 hectares, but I don't think I'll ever use it. The house is 150 kilometres from the centre of the district, and there are no roads, trains or buses. People still live off their garden produce and their cows; they sell milk to the state at a ridiculously low price, without the slightest hope of a better life.

As for me, life with my grandmother enabled me to recover from the nervous exhaustion caused by the never-ending rows at home. At the end of my studies, I won the gold medal and entered Khmelnytskyi University to study accounting. In those years, it was prestigious to become an economist, lawyer or accountant. So I followed the trend without knowing that it wasn't my real calling. Of course, I had to pay the fees. For the first two years, my mother helped me. Then I moved on to a correspondence course and started working to pay for myself.

In my first year, I loved the humanities, philosophy, cultural history and the history of religions – but political economy and basic economics also interested me. What I missed was social activity. At school, I'd been on the students' committee and showed a good deal of inventiveness in organizing concerts and events. In college, there was just a student committee which, once a year, organized a Students' Day. It was a real wasteland! To fill this gap, I suggested to my philosophy teacher that she should organize a society for discussing ideas. Only ten students signed up out of the whole university, and the society lasted only three months.

In the second year, when we began to study accounting, I realized that the profession I'd chosen wasn't the right one for me. Debit and credit frankly made me sick. I systematically skipped those courses, and was eventually expelled for my unjustified absences. Mom made me promise to get my degree, and so I humbly asked to be reinstated. As it was a paying course, this wasn't very difficult. In short, I was expelled and then let back in, ten times over. Once, I even sat ten examinations and twelve re-takes in one week!

In the third year, while I was pursuing my correspondence courses, I worked on a market selling sweets and biscuits. Every day, I opened my booth at 6 a.m., lugged heavy boxes around, and laid out different candies. It wasn't an easy job but now I'm an expert in cakes and sweets. In the evening, after this exhausting work, I attended a philosophical circle in the courtyard of a building on Dubov Street, to which my girlfriends Lena and Ira had taken me. I often fell asleep in the middle of discussions because I was tired all the time. I decided to seek less physical work that would leave me with enough energy to cultivate myself. I found a job as a secretary, thanks to the computer skills I'd learned at university.

This philosophical circle influenced me a lot. There were high-school pupils fourteen to fifteen years old and students of eighteen or nineteen, but also an adult, Maxim, who was thirty-five. All these very different people had found common ground, thanks to our Marxist mentor, Viktor Svyatski who became my very close friend. In the courtyard there was a large wooden table round which the neighbours used to gather to sip beer. But we took it over to read works of philosophy aloud and discuss them, much to the hilarity of the inhabitants. In winter, we gathered in small groups, sometimes in one person's home, sometimes in another's, but the cold didn't interrupt our activities. It was such an unmissable educational experience for all of us. Before joining this discussion group, we'd all been leading aimless lives, and our parents didn't have any authority in our eyes. Lost in this new post-Soviet, capitalist world, where you had to fight to survive, they had nothing to pass on to us. In our discussion group, we discovered Marxism and made real friends.

Why Marxism? We liked the idea that people are born equal and should remain so. The idea that everyone can develop his abilities, his creativity, instead of having to submit to the fate that capitalist society imposes on him. We also had a certain nostalgia for the Soviet Union. Stalinist repression belonged in the distant past, while the last Soviet decades appeared to us as a period of relative happiness. Of course, we were deluding ourselves, since the end of the Soviet regime had coincided with our childhood, and childhood, by definition, is a time of happiness. Anyway, each of us found it difficult to cope with unfettered capitalism, myself included. My father was out of work, my mother had become a poor peasant, I had to work in the market to pay for my studies while some students, children of the nouveau riche, came to college in cars purchased by their parents. But my parents weren't duffers. It was unfair that some were getting richer while others were social rejects!

Yet to begin with, when I was asked to join a left-wing philosophical circle, my first reaction was: 'You're crazy Commies!' I was then immediately shown that the Soviet system had nothing to do with Marxist theory. We read philosophy textbooks but we also went back to the sources, studying Marx, Hegel or Engels. Of course we read *Capital*, and it helped me a lot in college. We were also very excited about Italian Marxism and were wildly enthusiastic about the Red Brigades. It was so romantic!

By reading these authors, I became a convinced atheist. Throughout my childhood and even still in college, I habitually said my prayers before going to bed. My grandmother had taught me how to pray and I reckoned that if I stopped, I'd be struck by lightning. When I gained a better understanding of the history of the world and mankind, and the true function of religion, I also realized that God didn't exist. That was how it was, and not otherwise. One day, as usual, I knelt down to say my evening prayers, but I immediately stood up again and went to bed. Since then, I've never prayed or crossed myself.

Studying Marxism, we kept wondering what we could do to change our lives. This led us to design the Centre for Youth Opportunities, meant to serve as an interface between the demands of students from various institutions of higher learning, and their administrations. In short, we wanted to fight for the rights of students and contribute to their intellectual development.

I worked as a secretary for a certain Olga Ivanovna Ugrak, a wealthy woman who ran an auditing firm. She was atypical, different from other nouveau riche because she devoted her free time to social work on behalf of large families and orphans. It was she who provided us with a place for our organization and helped us to register it officially. However, this activity wasn't enough for me, and in our circle, I was perceived as an unstable person. Seeking my path, I had waxed enthusiastic in turn about philosophy, then political economy and history. I was wildly enthusiastic about each discipline, then I dropped it. The discovery of feminism helped me set myself a lasting goal.

Basically, I was already a feminist without knowing it. The example of my parents traumatized me: how could my mother have married a man because he was a good dancer? The fact that most of my girlfriends had married right after high school shocked me deeply. Their parents did not seem to think that they should first allow their daughters to go to college or to find a proper job. In my village, all those girls who got married so young are already divorced, and they each have two or three children. And these children are having more children! These young women quickly lose interest in their kids, especially if they re-marry. The children grow up on the street. At the age of three, they're already using four-letter words and making the drunkards laugh. It's scandalous: children that nobody wants, that nobody cares about. In the towns, it's the same. I remember one Saturday when I was watching newly wed couples coming out of the town hall in Khmelnytskyi. The girls looked to be sixteen or seventeen years. I said to myself: poor young women! Their lives are already over, they won't go to college, they'll have kids and won't be able to work. And in three or four years, when love's flown out of the window, they'll be out on the streets perhaps, with their kids. If early marriage destroys a woman's life, it enhances the man's social status. He'll continue to go out with his friends, he'll be able to work, to study, but he'll be considered a serious fellow because he wears a wedding ring on his finger. That's the difference in social status!

I spoke to my friends about my discovery – the way it's really the woman who is devoid of any protection in society! But no one took me seriously. I began to educate myself, and I quickly realized that what interested me and moved me most was the status of women in our society. The struggles of our Centre for Youth Opportunities, such as the fight against the reduction in student scholarships, suddenly seemed futile in the face of this problem. Moreover, discrimination existed even within our Centre: even though it was mostly the girls who worked uncomplainingly, there were only men at the top of the hierarchy.

I finally found some girls in the centre who shared my concerns. I suggested we hold closed sessions, for women only, based on the slogan: 'All men are bastards'. This was a good way of letting off steam. We had to get the image of our enemy right in our sights. We discussed examples from our everyday lives: we analysed the behaviour of our fathers, our boyfriends, our superiors. At the same time, we read August Bebel's *Women and Socialism*[1] to integrate our observations within a theoretical framework. It was during these meetings that I met Sasha, brought along by an activist at the centre, Irina Serbina. Poor Sasha initially thought that we were crazy! As for Oksana, she was already present, but at that time was preoccupied by her artistic projects.

We finally came up with the idea of creating a purely women's group, Women's Initiative, as a rejection en bloc of everything male. This decision caused a split in the Centre for Youth Opportunities and our new group left after a big argument. Once we'd separated from the men, we took the name of 'New Ethics'. It was Olga Ivanovna, my boss, who again helped us to register this new group.

Nevertheless, I kept a few friends, and in particular Viktor. Despite his initial scepticism, we gradually convinced him of the need to fight for women's rights. His arguments were simple: 'Women have no future! To begin with, they're never on time for anything!'

Our group got off to a difficult start. Nobody wanted to support us, and my idea was seen as yet another transient craze. After two months of not getting very far, I was even ready to dissolve the organization because several girls had left. Yet I did organize conferences and debates on discrimination against women, in five universities. For me, this was a way of honing my skills and learning to argue with a sometimes hostile male audience. These conferences, which threw a damning light on the female condition, attracted a good number of girls into our ranks.

So we continued our discussions at meetings of the New Ethics group. In addition to Bebel's book – our Bible – we carefully studied an anthology of work on gender theory that gave us a good idea of bourgeois feminism. Bebel himself didn't really have a theory as such, but his book is an extraordinary history of women through the ages, and this reading confirmed us in our intuitions. We also read a Ukrainian feminist, Solomiya Pavlichko,[2] and then we each educated ourselves as much as we could. Today we are much more critical of our readings, we just help ourselves to whatever we need. But at the time, our ideology wasn't yet formed, we only knew that we needed to fight for women's rights, and in particular for their education.

To 'wake up' women students a bit, give them more confidence, we invented a contest called Brain Ring, a kind of intellectual competition. It took us two months to form five or six teams of women students from different universities. The majority of them seemed sceptical. 'Oh, but we're stupid, we could never take part in such a thing!' That was the reply we always got. We had to be patient and convince them that they were intelligent and well able to play the game. We even got students of the masculine gender to serve us glasses of water and distribute the sheets of paper during the competitions!

I continued to work for Olga Ivanovna, devoting all my free time to New Ethics. Then, in 2006, my boss decided to stand in the municipal elections. So I found myself getting dragged into an election campaign – an invaluable experience that allowed me to discover the repellent underbelly of Ukrainian politics. Olga Ivanovna did not skimp on resources. She even invited spin doctors to come from

Moscow and St Petersburg. At that time, before the financial crisis, the candidates spent money without a second thought, on billboards and leaflets, for instance. However, neither the Russian gurus nor the huge sums invested were of any help: Olga Ivanovna lost, and suffered a serious nervous breakdown.

I immediately lost my job with her, and since I'd just got my degree in accountancy, I had to decide what to do with my life. I needed to earn a living, and to help our movement develop. I gradually realized that Khmelnytskyi was too narrow a framework. For example, we were on very good terms with the head of Family Affairs and Youth in the regional Soviet; we organized concerts and meetings together, and he even got small grants for our actions, but it didn't help things move along. Indeed, we risked being transformed into an annex of the municipal authority that was still very Soviet. Real life was happening elsewhere – in Kiev. Whether you wanted to make a film or start a women's movement, that's where you had to go. I made my mind up.

I already knew Kiev, but I didn't like it – it was a noisy, restless city. Nevertheless, at the end of 2007, I packed my bags and arrived in the capital. I found a job as manager in show business and this experience taught me a lot, especially in the field of press relations. I was struck by the way it's possible to create an event out of nothing, once this 'nothing' looks good as a performance. I was also stunned to see how interested people can get in the brand of panties worn by a star actress, while some people focus on incomparably more interesting things – but nobody writes about them. For example, I was looking for women's associations in Kiev, but I could find only one. It was led by three glum matrons and was shrouded in total anonymity. As I was intent on continuing with New Ethics, I told myself we had to do everything we could to gain in notoriety. For this, we needed to grab media attention. The problem was that journalists don't come rushing along when you announce a conference on the prospects of gender studies in Ukraine. That's when I had the idea of introducing performances into our protests. The gestation of Femen had begun.

3

SASHA, THE SHY ONE

I was born in Khmelnytskyi in 1988. I spent my early childhood in East Germany where my father, a professional soldier, was stationed. We returned to Ukraine after the breakup of the USSR and the withdrawal of Soviet troops. My father left the army because he could not stand the way it had become debased. He explained that he couldn't continue when he didn't have enough to feed his soldiers. Thus he ended his career with the rank of captain. In the 1990s, he embarked on a business career.

We lived with my maternal grandparents. Every morning at dawn, my mother and grandmother cooked meat pies, and Grandmother would sell them at the market. Meanwhile, Mom sold jeans. As for Dad's business, I don't know exactly what it was, but it meant he constantly had to travel. We didn't have a phone at home, and there were no mobiles in those days. So we never knew where Dad was. Mom worried continuously about him.

My parents got along well. I was a single child and I

dreamed of having a brother or sister. My parents had nothing against the idea, but it didn't work out. After a few years,
my father managed to raise enough money to buy us an
apartment in the same building as my grandparents. Today,
most of the family is reunited: my parents, my mother's twin
brother and my maternal grandparents. They get together
regularly: a real tribe. Only my paternal grandparents live far
away, in the south of Ukraine. My father was born in the far
north, in Anadyr. His parents had been lured there by the
high wages, and this is where they met. Dad left Anadyr to
go to a military school in Ukraine, but his parents remained
in the north until the collapse of the USSR. After forty years
of life in the north, they wanted to spend their old age in a
warmer climate.

I don't have any particularly traumatic memories of my
childhood. We had a hard life in the early years of independence, but everyone was in the same boat. At school, I was an
excellent student but, in college, a gang of students began
to harass me. They first set their sights on another girl who
ended up attempting suicide, and then they hounded me. I
was forced to move to another class. I still don't know why
they decided to pick on me. We had a young woman as our
form tutor; she was a bit loopy and didn't pay much attention to the pupils, which didn't help things. When I joined
another class in the same school, the atmosphere was very
different. In the first two weeks, the whole class went out of
its way to welcome the new pupils so they wouldn't feel like
intruders or feel scared.

However, the persecution I had suffered left its traces.
I continued to work hard but I became shy. I always knew
the answers to the teachers' questions but I was afraid
to put my hand up. Reciting poems aloud was torture. I
always hoped that the lesson would end before I was called
up to the blackboard. Only when I started in the sixth

form did I finally become freer and my life a bit more cheerful.

Perhaps this feeling of freedom also came from the Orange Revolution. Khmelnytskyi is in Western Ukraine and our teachers, most of whom supported Yushchenko, allowed us to miss school to go on demonstrations. We were so happy to spend hours on the main square of the town, with our orange ribbons! Even my parents, who had lived in Russia and weren't mad keen on the Ukrainian mentality, took part in collecting money and clothing for Orange supporters. Truckloads of warm clothes and blankets were sent from Khmelnytskyi to Kiev, so that the people on the Maidan would not get cold. This revolution seemed such a pure, decent and fair event to us, it was impossible not to support it.

This breath of freedom, this joy of being together, with our friends – it was extraordinary. During the revolution, those on the 'Orange' side felt a sense of unity that made them throw out their shoulders and stand tall. Everyone greeted you with a smile. We felt like brothers, the radiance of people was beautiful to see. But the supporters of the 'Blues' looked dreadful, worn out, like alcoholics sometimes are. They came out on the counter-demonstrations not out of any enthusiasm but because they were paid to do so!

Unfortunately, our momentum was quickly broken. I don't accuse Yushchenko for having compromised the revolution. The Ukrainians are just as guilty as the 'Orange power'. People needed to claim control of power and to fight for essential reforms. If we ourselves don't make a move, how can we expect everything to be handed to us on a plate?

I left school having passed my final exams at seventeen, without any idea of what I wanted to do with my life. I understood that it wouldn't be possible to enjoy a good college education at Khmelnytskyi, simply because the university system is totally corrupt. Talented, ambitious people don't want to go into teaching because it's not a prestigious profession. So it's very mediocre or downright incompetent teachers who take the classes, especially when it's young teachers we're talking about.

My parents suggested I should join the Interregional Academy for Staff Management. The title certainly sounds imposing but in reality, the teaching there is rather poor, with the exception of a few professors. However, my parents had another motivation. They said that the academy was attended by children from good families and that I'd find a husband there. I followed their advice, but not with the aim of getting married. I wanted something else, though I didn't know what. My desires were still unclear. At home, we had the great classics of youth from the Soviet period. When I read them, I regretted not having been a Pioneer or a member of the Komsomol. I envied my parents, who'd gone to summer camps for Pioneers and done Komsomol work experience, instead of spending their time smoking and drinking beer in the yard, like people my age. This is a very serious problem in Ukraine: young people do not have enough to occupy their free time. A few years later, while I was in jail for a few days following a Femen action, I shared my cell with some girls who were drug addicts and had been stealing. Beautiful girls – they said they'd started sniffing and later shooting up, they were so bored. Now it was difficult for them to stop. It wasn't any tragedy in their families that had driven them to drugs, just boredom.

Of course, in Khmelnytskyi in the 1990s and early 2000s, there were branches of political parties and all kinds of associations, but I wasn't aware of their existence. I had just one girlfriend, Irina Serbina, two years younger than me. For years, we went around together, without joining the gangs of young people drinking, smoking and sniffing. One day when I was seventeen and already in the first year of college, we

were accidentally lured into a cult. A teacher at my university
told us that a drama circle was meeting in the basement of
a church, and this circle was recruiting new members. Irina
and I were welcomed by a very fanatical woman who was a
cunning psychologist. Despite our almost immediate desire
to escape, she was able to convince us, in one evening, that
we were the chosen of the Lord. For six months, we wore
black skirts, white blouses and white scarves. The teacher
in question also attended the sect. My parents were happy.
Their daughter went to church every Sunday, and brought
back the blessed bread; she knew how to pray and cross
herself – so everything was fine.

In fact, all of this just laid the base for our future mission. Shortly after, we were asked to attend prisons to recite
religious texts and then maintain a correspondence with
the prisoners. Irina, my friend, rebelled and left the sect. I
was uncomfortable. How could I leave since I'd accepted
the mission? It was my mother who put the kibosh on my
commitment; she didn't want me to come into contact with
the prison world.

The place I found myself in next was even more dangerous than a cult. Irina and I were looking for a new job, and
a girl in college told me that I could become a top model
because I was tall. OK, I thought, I'll give it a go! We took
part in the show of a local TV channel in Khmelnytskyi, and
a week later a man called and invited me to a nightclub to
attend a 'beauty and talent contest'. Why not, I asked myself.
But it was horrible! We were supposed to walk among the
tables all night long, putting up with the dirty comments
the guys made about us, all for the modest sum of fifty
hryvni. After an hour, I ran away with another girl, and that
was the end of my modelling career.

Six months later, a girlfriend from college told me about a
student organization where interesting things were happen-

ing and where students were given help. It was the Centre
for Youth Opportunities. So Irina and I went to a meeting
where there were only girls. We were seated in a large circle.
We discussed specific cases. Every girl told her story – how
one had been abused by her boyfriend, another by her father,
and so on. Anna, who hosted the meeting, tried to focus negative emotions on the opposite sex and explained that the
case studies were glaring demonstrations of the inequality
between men and women. However, she carefully avoided
the term 'feminism'. The girls were convinced that feminism
was a hobby for mad, moustachioed women, whereas what
they wanted was to get married and have a normal life. In
fact, we were witnessing the very last meeting in the centre.
At this meeting, it was decided to create a women's organization, New Ethics. We voted for this resolution, but simply
so as not to seem out of place. This hour of discussion on the
theme 'all men are bastards' hadn't convinced us. We didn't
have the experience that would allow us to share this view.

On the way back, we told each other that once again we'd
fallen among crazy folk. Yet we decided to go back, just to
make sure. Gradually, we started to get really enthusiastic.
These girls weren't crazy. They discussed the female condition to put it in a historical and political context, not simply
to draw a line under personal insults they'd suffered. From
time to time, they also invited along guys who had nothing
against feminism, to hear their points of view. Gradually, the
scales fell from our eyes.

We started to read and learn almost by heart August
Bebel's *Women and Socialism*. It was exciting because we'd
never heard anything about the hidden history of women.
We were so thrilled that we started to talk to female friends
and strangers about it: 'You know that, earlier, there was
matriarchy, women's rights, a matrilineal system, etc?
And afterwards, men, those bastards, took everything for

themselves because they wanted to transmit their property just to their biological children.' In short, we poured out such a torrent of words on the women we buttonholed that they replied: 'No, I don't want to join your organization.' We were going about it the wrong way but we felt that if we told the truth, they'd understand us. We organized trips for children, students and schools, and I felt involved and useful to society.

It was in New Ethics that I met Oksana and Anna. That's also where I discovered the world of voluntary associations. It was a radically different environment from nationalist groups or student committees, whose members used them to get good exam results and not because they wanted to fight for the rights of students. As for the political parties, even when I learned of their existence, they didn't attract me. I felt there was too much monkey business in each party, and too little concern for the public good.

When New Ethics broke away from the Centre for Youth Opportunities, almost all the girls followed Anna. But gradually, only the most motivated remained.

For over a year, we held our meetings in Viktor's kitchen, reading Bebel and other authors, but we eventually realized that we had to do something because our circle wasn't growing. It wasn't difficult to bring new recruits to our meetings, but most dropped out quickly because what we were doing was complicated and of little interest to more than a few. If we'd read *Vogue*, we'd have been much more popular. It was then that we realized we needed to develop simpler and more understandable means of attracting girls to feminism.

We decided to set up competitions called Brain Rings for the female students. Two teams immediately wanted to participate: the team from the Pedagogical Institute where, with few exceptions, there were only women students, and another composed of former members of the Centre for

Youth Opportunities. But we struggled to recruit eight more teams. We told them: 'It's simple, we need to form a team of six girls, you come on the right day and time, you sit at the table and you play. We take care of the organization.' But the students were very reluctant; they worried they wouldn't be up to it intellectually.

This is how the game was played: we would get together ten teams from different higher-educational institutions. The presenter would read the question and give a minute for people to answer. He then collected the papers with the answers – one for each team – and gave them to the commission. Then they would start again. At the end of the competition, the commission would announce the correct answers and the results, depending on the number of points obtained. Of course, the questions were on female themes so as to arouse the interest of the teams and the audience in this topic.

In the end, this women's Brain Ring lasted for five years – three years after Anna and I left for Kiev. The competition became a brand for the student youth in town, so popular that some clubs and cafes even sponsored it. The league, which had enabled many women to learn about feminism, ceased to exist only a year ago.

As we read Bebel in Viktor's kitchen, we had to put up with teasing from the guys in the Centre for Youth Opportunities that we'd left. 'Well then, ladies, what do you think you would achieve? You're going nowhere fast!' For a whole year, we convinced ourselves that we could achieve something without their help. We taught ourselves to observe a discipline that had hitherto been completely lacking. For example, if a kitten came into the kitchen, all the girls began to fidget: 'Oh, the little kitty!' and they forgot Bebel and why we were reading him. They'd seen the cat, and they got all excited. Or, if there were young men dropping by at Viktor's, they suddenly turned all flirtatious: 'Why hello, guys!' We were trying to get rid of all this feminine silliness.

On 9 May 2007,[1] at the annual contest for activists in the different parties and organizations in Khmelnytskyi, we formed our own column. The Centre for Youth Opportunities, which was declining, had formed a column too, with boys and girls. Ours was bigger and all the girls were beautiful, carrying pennants, shouting slogans and hailing the veterans. We won the contest, and the guys from the Centre recognized that we were the best and that the 'ladies' were able to organize themselves! For us, it was a matter of honour – we wanted to know whether or not we were able to act without being told what to do by men.

In autumn of the same year, we also attempted a first action. In Khmelnytskyi, two women had died in the hospital due to nurses who had inadvertently given them enemas with formalin! In fact, errors of this kind happen daily in Ukraine, but in general, nobody is informed and those responsible are never punished. However, journalists picked up rumours of the case, and it caused a big scandal. We spent half a day in the rain and the snow, wearing bloodied sheets as banners and placards: 'Who's next?' In the evening, the governor received us in person and promised he would punish all the guilty.

On this occasion we became acquainted with a pathologist who knew what city hospitals were like. He told us of a case where an incompetent surgeon had removed a patient's uterus instead of her appendix! He was trying to encourage the relatives of those who had died due to the incompetence of medical staff to complain, so as to prevent those people from continuing to work. In 2007, he was at the end of his tether. He'd suffered assassination attempts and wanted to stop practising, for he saw that he could never get justice done, due to the corruption of the judicial system.

For us, the lesson of that day of struggle was different. We realized that our actions could attract media attention and, just as importantly, we were able to act as a united front. The staff responsible for the error, and the Chief Medical Officer and duty intern, were dismissed, although I can't say that this was only due to our action. In any case, we had fanned the flames. This action marked the beginning of Femen in Khmelnytskyi.

By this time, Anna had already gone to Kiev. The rest of us continued our readings and actions in Khmelnytskyi, but we knew that it was impossible to realize our dream in a small provincial town, where there were only three newspapers and one local TV channel. We had crazy plans to conquer Ukraine and for that we needed to act in Kiev.

My girlfriend Irina had also gone to study in Kiev. The first six months, she hung out in clubs for fun, and didn't get involved in social activism. However, she soon found that this was even more annoying than our activities in Khmelnytskyi. Thus, she and Anna began to recruit new girls and Femen soon become operational.

4

OKSANA, THE ICONOCLAST

Mom grew up in an orphanage. She always dreamed of having a family, of being a mother. After leaving high school, she didn't want to continue with her education. She married at eighteen and gave birth to me the following year. My father and she made a happy couple. Three years later, Lyosha, my brother was born. We were both loved and cared-for children. My father worked at the factory; he was a good mechanic. My parents wanted to have more children, but for this, they had to buy an apartment and earn a good living. However, after the collapse of the USSR, these plans proved impossible. The factory closed, my father was made redundant and he began to drink. Mom started to go out to work to ensure our survival.

Khmelnytskyi is a town with one of the largest markets in Europe. More than half of the population makes a living in it. Mom resold goods purchased from wholesalers. I remember that every day, early in the morning, we would go to the market with Lyosha in his pram. Mom unfolded a sheet and laid it on the ground to set out her articles. When we came back from the market, my father was already dead drunk. Mom didn't want to walk out on him, he was the only man in her life, and she always hoped he'd conquer his weakness. The problem was that he didn't have the will to work, not even helping Mom. At this level, women are stronger and more resilient, as they have the maternal instinct and a sense of duty. My father could have found some sort of job, but he was a broken man. Mom still doesn't want to leave him because she thinks he'd die without her. Today, he's a sick man, totally unbalanced.

There was a period in my life, between the ages of eight and twelve years, when I tried to get him to stop drinking. I begged him, I made a nuisance of myself, I screamed, but this just irritated him. He raised his hand to me several times. On various occasions, he was put into a clinic for the treatment of alcoholism, but the respite was short-lived. Mom was destroyed by grief and kissed the rest of her life goodbye. She's a very religious woman, and she would never have dreamt of finding herself another husband. For her, a church wedding means marriage for life.

Around the age of fifteen, I started to persuade her that she'd fulfilled her maternal duty and that she should live for herself. Gradually, this pressure changed her. She believes that I helped her to stand firm and she's very proud of me. She even says that I'm the pivot of her existence and that I gave her a new lease of life. Even if she still lives with my father, out of pity but also recognizing that he gave her children, she has become an independent and confident woman. She now works in a shop selling tools and building materials. She's capable of carrying on very professional discussions with her customers, about nuts or drills.

I always wanted to become an artist. From my earliest childhood, drawing was my favourite occupation. When a studio for icon painting opened in Khmelnytskyi, I wanted to attend. The teacher himself had been trained in Greece, on Mount Athos. My father took me there but the teacher said he only took students who were at least twenty years old. I was eight! Canonical Byzantine painting on wooden board, using precious metals, is very complicated and meticulous work, which requires you to have had an artistic training. The teacher advised my father to register me in a drawing studio for children, but my father begged him, and refused to leave. So, to get rid of us and to show my father I was useless, the teacher gave me some tests to do. But when he saw my work, he remained speechless. He told my father that I had a heaven-sent gift, and he took me on as a student. Thus, from the age of eight, I started to paint icons and at the age of ten, I was already part of a group involved in decorating churches. I finished my apprenticeship at the age of fifteen.

My grandmother and my mother are very religious, Dad much less so. He didn't go to church, but he wasn't a militant atheist either. When I started painting icons, I immersed myself in reading the lives of the saints and the Gospels. I knew dozens of prayers by heart. I prayed morning and evening, before starting work and after I'd finished. I observed all the Church's rules, including fasting. I was so skinny that my mother told me: 'Do stop, you'll kill yourself!' But I fasted, I went to church, I went to confession, I went to Sunday school. I was so immersed in religion that, at the age of thirteen, I decided to enter a convent. I packed my bag and I was about to leave when Mom unexpectedly returned home, at lunch time. She asked me: 'Where are you going?'

'I'm entering a convent. I want to seek God and devote my life to him. I want to pray for you. And after my death, I'll live in heaven.'

Mom was appalled. I was a very independent child and I

always finished what I started. So she called on our whole extended family for help, and everyone implored me not to go into the convent. It would be better for me to get married and have children and grandchildren.

This prompted me to think seriously about God and faith. I wondered what religion really means if those who seem to believe in God and instil this faith in their children are at the same time afraid to entrust these children to God.

I suddenly rebelled against traditional religion. I admit that there may be a supreme intelligence, but in any case, I gave up any religious practice. I also mulled over my years in the icon studio. I thought about how priests came to see us and haggled over the price of our work like carpet sellers. About the fact that they gave us nothing to eat while we were working on frescoes, saying that God would reward us. The way they got up to all sorts of petty tricks . . .

Once I'd left the workshop, I started taking commissions for icons, but only so I could make a living. In Ukraine, there's a well-established tradition: people aren't satisfied with copies you can buy in shops, but they commission icons from skilled artists for church weddings, baptisms or important events. Those who can afford it don't skimp on resources because they want icons of high quality that they will leave as a legacy to their children.

As a teenager, I began to reflect on the meaning of my life. What is my place on Earth? Do I have a mission to accomplish? What can I do to fight injustice? It was at this time that I got to know Anna Hutsol and the guys from a philosophical circle that met in the street. We read books and discussed the great philosophical questions. There were some older boys who taught us many things while continuing to learn for themselves. We started off with general concepts – what are philosophy, metaphysics and dialectics? When we started, we used a philosophy textbook from the Soviet era, a kind of overview of the history of philosophy. Then we moved on to more complicated texts. I dutifully read the first two volumes of Marx's *Capital*, but I have to admit I couldn't get through the third.

I felt a huge yearning for freedom. I wanted to free myself from all these standards of behaviour imposed by society. When I was fourteen, I met some young people on the fringes of society, hippies and punks, and I started to hang out with them. They were cultured and intelligent teenagers, but they were a bit lost and were trying to find themselves in underground movements. When I discovered the philosophical circle, I dragged quite a few people from that milieu along. Most found some answers to their questions. I have two friends in particular, Fyodor and Den, who subsequently went to Chernivtsi to study philosophy – they're currently doing PhDs.

Yes, we were punks, but we were thinking about things and we wanted to fight against this false system. The capitalist state dictates the rules of our lives: you come into the world, you study at school, then university, you start a family, you have kids and you work. Your salary is just enough for you to pay for rent and utilities, and feed your family. Actually, it's a pale imitation of real life, a mere reproduction of the labour force! But we want each individual to start to think, to be able to become a philosopher or poet. People are all born equal and are designed to be creative. Everything depends on their education and the conditions in which they live.

Today, the philosophical circle no longer exists. We've all grown up. But there's now a 'street university' in Khmelnytskyi, where some of my friends work with the new generation. In summer, they gather once or twice a week in a park, give lectures and invite specialists from all over Ukraine, sometimes from Russia or other countries, to give lectures.

After college, I went to a technology high school to learn how to use graphics software. I knew I wouldn't be able to become a graphic designer without going to a school, whereas I could continue to teach myself to be an artist and painter. This school was a funny place where you worked all day, like in a factory, from 8 a.m., with a lunch break. That's when I decided to live away from my parents.

I moved into a clay cottage that had belonged to my grandfather. There wasn't any toilet or running water but there was electricity and gas. The cottage was in very poor nick. To make it livable in, I had to learn how to wield an axe and other tools. I even managed to set up my studio in it. After high school, I decided I'd educate myself because the education system was rotten. The worst thing is that it didn't allow the student's personality to be developed: instead, they did everything to stifle it. As for the painting of icons, this was my livelihood, but I did the bare minimum, just to have something to eat. I didn't want be a burden on my mother.

My studies at the technological school lasted three years. It was difficult but I got my degree. I knew Anna from our philosophy circle, and then I met Sasha. Anna, Viktor and I created the Centre for Youth Opportunities, where we tried to defend student rights. Our trio from Khmelnytskyi, Anna, Sasha and myself, really started to come together in New Ethics, the first movement for girls that we didn't wish to view as a feminist movement. At the time, the term seemed confused and derogatory. We shared out the roles quite naturally: Anna was the organizer, Sasha the spokesperson, and I was the artist and designer. The idea was simple, we needed to prove to ourselves as well as others that we women were not any dumber than men. We gave lectures in universities, organized Brain Ring sessions, helped out at orphanages. That's what we busied ourselves with between 2006 and 2008.

It was a difficult period, for social activism was very dimly viewed in our town. People couldn't understand why we were doing that, and we had to face a lot of prejudice. When I was at school, my mother kept telling me all the time: 'What's the point of all that? You study, you go to the icon workshop, you do sport. That's enough!' The reaction of my teachers was similar; they thought I was wasting my time with fads. Even my friends had trouble understanding me, and kept suggesting I should have a few beers or go and see a film.

There were between fifty and a hundred of us in New Ethics. However, we needed to grow and, more than anything, conquer the capital. In 2008, we changed the name to Femen. Anna moved to Kiev, then Sasha joined her. I went to Kiev only two years ago. I had stayed in Khmelnytskyi because of my studio – I couldn't move with all my equipment.

In addition to the icons, I also painted portraits and landscapes to order. In Khmelnytskyi, I put on several exhibitions, but since my move to Kiev, I've devoted myself entirely to our movement. Our messages and protests are what matters most to me. Real art is the revolution. It's this art that wakes people up and encourages them to reflect on their lives and the world. I was still planning to have an exhibition in Kiev, with the paintings I'd left behind in Khmelnytskyi, but six months ago, my parents' apartment where they were stored burned down. Everything I'd created was destroyed by fire. I have quality photos of only 10 percent of the pictures. Too bad, it's nothing. I'll paint more works. Sooner or later, I'll get back to painting.

Part II

ACTION

5

'UKRAINE IS NOT A BROTHEL'

A SOFT-CORE START

In spring 2008, Anna began to organize meetings in her Kiev apartment, with Irina Serbina and some other girls she'd met in Kiev. Initially, Sasha and Oksana were still shuttling between Khmelnytskyi and Kiev. Anna was looking for a name for our movement because New Ethics was too academic. It was by chance that she found one on the Internet: *femen* is 'thigh', a variation of *femur* in Latin, but it's like the French word *femme* for woman, and it sounds good. In any case, our friend Viktor, who worked in advertising, approved!

However, Sasha and Oksana were resolutely against it and proposed the name 'Amazons'. After a month of discussions, we finally adopted Femen, in Roman characters. The name is short and mysterious, its five letters enable it to be used effectively in graphic terms, and it has a hard sound – because we want to be hard.

When we started, our feminist movement defined itself

as the negation of all that is masculine. Little by little, our thinking has matured and we understand that the enemy is not a particular man. The enemy is the general pattern of patriarchy. There are nice people among the men! Like Viktor, who is perfectly at ease with feminism. Moreover, when he's not travelling, he's glad to help us.

Our first steps were very theatrical. We had some striking costumes and even invited women starting out as singers or dancers to join us in small productions. On the Day of the Earth, for example, we wore pink jackets, and inflated thirty balloons – also pink – and released them. There was no media presence. Today, it all seems cheesy and naive, but what mattered to us was to get out on to the streets. We needed to break through this mental barrier and become a 'public' group.

We didn't immediately find anything that would motivate us to demonstrate. Then, after two tragic suicides in the metro, we came up with the idea of a 'Positive Metro'. This initiative took place in July 2008. We inflated some balloons, bought sweets, drew banners and went down into the metro, calling on people to show respectful and friendly behaviour. We also demanded that a special compartment should be created for women who were pregnant or travelling with children. Admittedly, this action didn't have much to do with feminism, but for the first time, the press was there. When reporters asked us for a press release, we didn't even know what that was. So we learnt from this experience and, most importantly, we took the contact details of the journalists present. This action was important for us. We learned how to mobilize and prepare our little performance most effectively. Anna had previously agreed on our route with the management of the Kiev metro, and at the stations where we changed line, they stationed employees to welcome us and accompany us. The action was very well organized, and that gave us confidence.

'EVERYONE INTO THE WATER'

Then we started using our sexuality on behalf of the feminist cause. One week after the 'Metro' action, we organized a protest against the hot-water cuts that afflicted entire neighbourhoods in the capital, including student residences, during the summer.[1] 'No tap water, let's have a wash on Maidan Square!' This was the slogan for our performance.

It was hot and the water was cut off. We set the date for our swim: 15 July 2008. It was a kind of flash mob; there were about sixty of us there. The girls brought basins, sponges and shower gels, and invited a few journalists, although we didn't have a real database. At the time indicated, 12.15 p.m., a crowd of journalists arrived – not just the Ukrainian press, but also agencies such as Reuters and Associated Press – and we didn't know how to react in their presence. Anna shouted, 'Everyone into the water!' We jumped into the fountain, some in swimsuits and others in their dresses, and we started to dance about, screaming and jumping. There were even journalists who joined us, it was fun!

For Ukraine, this performance was totally unprecedented. The journalists were flabbergasted and kept asking us questions: 'Who are you? A dance group? A choir? Who's your leader? Where do you get your funding?' It was funny to see how they wanted, at all costs, to find a sponsor or a 'guide' behind Femen. Anyway, we discovered that women protesting could arouse press interest so long as they put on a show. Journalists need something spectacular – they feed on scandal, sex, death.

However, without the press, we can do nothing. If we're not in the news, it's as if our action hasn't even happened. This is unfortunately what happens with the majority of NGO activities. The authority of the media confers significance on an event. Like it or not, it's the way things are.

After this splash-about on the Maidan, Sasha decided she wanted to devote herself entirely to our movement, build it up and develop it. In the autumn of 2008, she moved to Kiev.

Everyone loved this action in the fountain. True, Anna was kept for two hours at the police station for 'an offence against public order', but we were a sensation! Over the next four years, we bathed every summer in the Maidan fountain, on the anniversary of this first action.

For the first two years, we didn't take our clothes off. We put on shows, with many participants and a lot of different sets. Oksana did all the work on the stage sets. This is what she has to say now about that period and her work at the time:

The girls were sharing rooms, and I couldn't move in with them. So I commuted. Khmelnytskyi is 400 kilometres from Kiev and the ticket, with student reduction, cost peanuts. The hard bit was being shaken about all night long in the train, with the sets that I was lugging along with me, and having to take part in an action the next morning. And doing this two or three times a month. But our new life was so exciting!

At first, I myself wove our crowns of flowers from the cheapest material, namely, the artificial flowers they sell in cemeteries. For the banners, we used the remains of wallpaper rolls the girls salvaged from their student residences after the summer redecorations. Sometimes we needed a big piece of cardboard to cut out letters but we didn't have the means to buy one. I looked for my materials in the street and even in rubbish tips: crates, cartons, the dregs from tins of paint, and anything that could be used. Nobody ever made a fuss. As for the clothes for our theatrical actions, we pieced them together from what we had in our wardrobes. At first, we had very little in the way of

expenses. If we needed balloons, for example, or credit for
mobile phones, we all chipped in.

SEX SAFARIS

Very quickly, we passed on to more serious matters, as they
say. We started a long campaign with the slogan 'Ukraine
is not a brothel'. From having been a playful and gentle
movement, we evolved into a radical feminist movement.
Sometimes we feel like dumping the photos of our first
actions, with those pink balloons and splashing around in
fountains, but it's our history. At the beginning, we wanted
to please everyone; we thought women at least would like us
because we were defending their rights. The problem is that
from the moment we committed ourselves to campaigning
against prostitution, they started calling us prostitutes. Men
especially, but sometimes women too!

How did this campaign begin? One day, while we were
talking, someone asked, 'What bothers you the most?'
Every girl began to tell of her misadventures: how one
was approached in the street by Turks who grabbed at her
skirt, or how some Europeans offer cocktails in nightclubs
to seduce a young inexperienced girl. The Turks are less
wealthy, so they approach girls in the street, hoping for a
lucky break. The Italians, Americans, Germans and French
pick up girls at the hotel or go to a brothel. Each hotel has
its catalogue of 'services', with photos and descriptions of
what every girl can do, and the men can order the woman
they like.

Foreigners come here because they know that, in Ukraine,
there's a whole sex industry. Ukraine is the new Thailand and
it's a growing phenomenon. In Kiev or Odessa, with a thou-
sand dollars in his pocket, a man is a king. The sex industry
works like a fast-food restaurant, a kind of McDonald's. It's

easy and cheap. Incidentally, it's also exotic for foreigners because Ukrainian girls are often beautiful and naive.

Experienced Westerners do not even go to the brothel – why pay more? A foreigner who knows a little about local customs goes to a nightclub and offers to buy a girl a drink. He tells her he's in Kiev on business, and the girl starts dreaming that he's going to marry her and take her to Europe. A lot of girls feel they have no other option in life: they don't have money to study, and the only jobs they can get are unattractive ones where they are cruelly exploited and underpaid. Then they start hanging around in nightclubs, which are generally free for women, looking for a Prince Charming. And once the prince's prey is tipsy, he spends the night with her, gratis.

Sometimes these stories have a 'happy ending'. In Austria we met a Ukrainian woman who had placed her details in a dating agency. She married the first Austrian who wanted her. Does she even realize that this is also a kind of prostitution – only long term? In any case, she doesn't look happy, and doesn't seem to be in love with her husband. And yet most of our girls don't even have as much 'luck'!

In Ukraine, a single step can lead to prostitution. You just have to chat with a guy handing out flyers encouraging girls to work as 'hostesses'. You tell him OK, or you call the number indicated, and that's the end of your life. Inna can testify to the risk of getting trapped:

That's what happened to some of the pupils in my class. Like me, they came from small towns to study in Kiev, with the dream of becoming someone and getting a decent job. Eventually, their parents could no longer help them because life is very expensive in Kiev compared with the rest of the country, and rents especially are exorbitant. These girls were thus forced to look for work. After some bad experiences with crooked managers in restaurants or shops, they tried strip clubs – the primrose path to prostitution. Very quickly, they were taken over by pimps, and their fate was sealed.

The first action against sex tourism took place a month after the bathing event on the Maidan. We carried it out in Kreshtchatik,[2] the city's red-light district. Before our actions, the Ukrainian press had been up in arms over sex tourism in Thailand, but nobody talked about what happens in Ukraine itself. The phenomenon exists, the Mafia bosses earn millions in this way, our elected officials are aware of it, but nobody does anything. Our senior civil servants and MPs are owners of clubs and brothels where they offer a wide range of sexual services. We've taken part in journalists' investigations on the subject, and we can vouch for what we say.

There are two types of sex tourism. The first is buying a sex tour on the Internet. Whole busloads of Turks use this system. They're put up in the hotel where they are entitled to prostitutes and each evening they get taken to a different brothel. The second type is a safari through various nightclubs, the favourite pastime of many European tourists.

A few years ago, we conducted a survey with an institute of social studies, and it turned out that 70 per cent of prostitutes' clients were Turks. Why? Perhaps because of old traditions. In bygone days, the Turks used to buy or kidnap young Ukrainian girls for their harems. Today, Ukraine is still easily accessible and cheap.

Europeans are more perverse. They discovered Ukraine thanks to the abolition of visas under Yushchenko[3] and especially thanks to Euro 2012. Of course, abolishing visas was meant to develop tourism and open Ukraine to the Western world. Except that, in practice, this has contributed to the development of sex tourism. Foreign men here see pretty blondes in short skirts and high heels, dreaming of marrying a foreigner so as to leave this horrible country. How can they fail to take advantage?

It costs them much less than a trip to Thailand, and security is better. For one thing, Kiev is a civilized city, and, second, the police are corrupt and won't interfere with foreigners. This needs to be emphasized: many foreigners come to Ukraine not for prostitutes, but for girls who don't really know what's happening to them. For some, these traumatic experiences with foreign men who seduce them and then dump them the following day leave the door open to real prostitution.

The worst thing is that according to some NGOs – though there aren't any official statistics – many adolescent girls begin to engage in prostitution at the age of twelve or thirteen years. These are mostly girls from broken and poor families, often with single parents or alcoholic fathers, which have become very widespread since the breakup of the USSR. There are neither social institutions nor state agencies to help them or care for their children. True, parents receive benefits, but these are paltry. In contrast, the recruitment system for the prostitution networks is very well organized. It's a whole industry, with its publicity department and managers of human resources, able to recruit, in particular, barely pubescent teens.

BAN'KA

Inna joined us in the summer of 2009. She knew Sasha and Anna and occasionally came to meetings. We met at the Ban'ka cafe in an old Turkish bath, where the tea was cheap. For forty or so girls, we ordered three teas, and we could talk for hours, sipping these three cups.

'Ukraine is not a brothel' was the first action in which

Inna participated. It was a kind of street theatre, a cheerful free-for-all in the centre of Kiev. About seventy girls were present, maybe even more. They were divided into several groups: a fashion show, dancers, 'dolls', and a radical group. The girls dressed as dolls, with big ribbon bows on their heads, represented prostitutes. Indeed, they *are* dolls: you can buy them and sell them. The most radical group – in which Inna played a part – wore swimwear, also with ribbon bows sewn on. The girls in swimsuits kept screaming: 'Ukrainian women are not prostitutes.' The action took place peacefully; you couldn't call it a real protest yet. In fact, it was very pretty: ribbons, balloons and lots of people. In addition, the message was simple and clear. Pretty young girls looking like prostitutes, but wearing signs saying 'I'm not a prostitute'.

At first, then, we were rebelling against the perception that all Ukrainian women are prostitutes. If a young unmarried Ukrainian woman requests a visa for a Western country, she's likely to meet with a refusal. At the age of nineteen, Inna was denied a visa to Germany, where she'd been invited as a member of Femen. They literally whispered into her ear, in the consulate, that her motives were suspect. Of course, we wanted to restore the dignity of Ukrainian women!

The more we learnt about prostitution, the more disgusted we were, and really angry at the Ukrainian state. We decided to demand that it be completely banned. On paper, it's prohibited – the sex industry is prohibited, the whole sex business is prohibited. In actual fact, if there's a brothel next to a police station, the police won't raid it – quite the opposite, they'll protect it. If the police arrest a prostitute, this is either at the request of her pimp because she wants to dump him, or to increase the 'tax'. This business is growing every day.

How are we to solve this problem? We've given the matter a great deal of thought and studied the situation in other countries. We believe that the Swedish model is very effective. The Swedes have introduced legislation to criminalize the client. It's clear: the man who buys sexual services is committing a crime. Not the prostitute, who is always the victim; not the pimp, who always finds some loophole, but whoever fosters the development of this trade, that is, the client. This is not the complete answer to the problem but it's a major step in reducing prostitution. These men are cowards; they're scared that their wives, their partners, their mothers and their sisters will learn how they behave. It's different from boasting about their exploits in front of their friends!

Besides, why do men go with prostitutes? In most cases, it's not out of any sexual need as such. They do it to feel superior, because they want to humiliate. This is the height of sadism – humiliating a woman by buying her, and making her do everything she's asked, in exchange for a morsel of bread, because she needs to feed her children or pay for medicine for her dying mother. That's why this business thrives. Not because men are too lazy to court a woman and buy her a bunch of flowers, but because, with a prostitute, the most pathetic little man feels like an absolute master.

So we issued a proposal to criminalize the clients of the sex industry. A member of the Rada[4] prepared a Bill based on our proposal. In Ukraine, we're not an association or a recognized NGO; they've always refused to register us. However, our proposal was taken into account and our Bill was discussed in ministries, in the Rada, in political talk shows – everywhere! We did what nobody had yet done in Ukraine: we opened a public debate on the subject of prostitution and sex tourism. Everyone knew that it existed; everyone could see the brothels and the adverts for the 'clubs', but nobody wrote about it. If you search through the archives of the Ukrainian press for 2006–7, you won't find a single article on prostitution in Ukraine written by a local journalist.

FEMEN ON TV

In 2009, we managed to get on TV, on Savik Shuster's programme,[5] where we discussed the Bill on criminalizing clients of the sex industry. An MP who took part in this programme, Nestor Shufrych, told us: 'You can count on me, girls, I swear on my mother's head that in the next parliamentary session, we'll pass this Bill.' He even gave his phone number and for us it was simply amazing. Normally, inhabitants of the political Olympus are inaccessible to mere mortals. And here he was, he spoke to us, he shook hands with us and looked us straight in the eyes, as he made these promises. It was 2 October 2009, and the Bill was going to be voted on in Parliament four days later.

More than a month went by and 'our' Bill seemed to have evaporated. But we learned that Shufrych would again be a guest on the programme *Shuster Live* on 27 November 2009. We decided that Sasha would try to break into the studio during the broadcast. But how could she get in? Let's hear Sasha's account:

I decided to improvise. Upon entering the studio, I asked the guards to call one of the women who worked there, whose name I'd remembered from the last time, Olessia. I then jabbered something over the phone to convince her to come down and I said: 'As you'll remember, we're the Femen group. We were invited on to Shuster's programme and Shufrych promised us he'd pass a law against prostitution. I absolutely need to talk to him, during the commercial break, for example, it's very important.' Taken by surprise, she made me go to a small waiting room for those who'd come to accompany the guests. I stayed there two minutes, and then I went in search of the TV set. I had a crown of flowers on my head, I was wearing a T-shirt with the inscription: 'Ukraine is not a brothel' and I was holding a rolled-up banner under my arm. As Femen still wasn't very well known, the staff didn't identify me and didn't suspect anything. One minute before the live show went out, however, the entrances to the set were all blocked. The passages from the circle were barred by cameramen and their massive equipment. I was desperate. Suddenly, I saw the presenter come into the room through a small door, on one side. I did the same and I found myself in the antechamber of the set. A quiver went through me. *My God, this is the moment of truth*, I told myself. On the set, they were just finishing a link-up with another city. I feverishly unfolded my banner behind a small curtain, and as soon as they started to put out the show, I ran on to the middle of the set screaming: 'Don't believe those liars!' On the banner were written the words: 'Lies, coming to you live'. Everyone was in a state of shock, but the cameras continued to film.

Generally, when we prepare an action, we ensure that it will be filmed. If we realize that it won't be broadcast live, it's better to do nothing and wait for a more opportune moment. That's why I waited for the end of the link-up to pounce.

Bravely, Shuster, who is a head shorter than me, grabbed me by the hand and asked: 'What's happening? What are you doing here? Who are you?' I started to explain that this Shufrych had promised to make Bill No. 5223 into law, but nothing had been done. I shouted: 'We won't stand for it any longer, it's time for politicians to be held to account for their words!' And in a fit of anger, I leapt at Shufrych and started to hit him with the banner. It was all being filmed! But he didn't flinch, he just frowned and said: 'Calm down, young girl, calm down.' A woman MP sitting next to him was outraged: 'Young girl, there's no need for such a performance!' I then swung the banner at Shufrych's face and quietly left the room. This was before Yanukovych came to power and at that time, they didn't arrest you for just nothing. Need it be said that the Bill was never made law?

CUSTARD PIE

Shuster wasn't Sasha's first exploit. Her first arrest, just for a few hours, went back to March 2009. We were shocked at the book by a provocative writer, Oles Bouzina, *Women, Back to the Harems*, in which he calls women 'cockroaches' and other horrible names. Unfortunately, he's a very popular writer in Ukraine, who loves to tickle the nerves of the public. In particular, he's written biographies of Taras Shevchenko and Ivan Franko,[6] in which he praises their perverse relation to women and their cruelty. This misogynist is very proud of his attitude, and we decided that he should be publicly punished.

We went to the launch of his new book in a Kiev bookshop, and when he started talking about this hateful book, Sasha dashed over to him and hurled a custard pie at his face. The guy reacted really violently. He caught Sasha and began to spray tear gas from a canister at the journalists who were photographing the scene. The director and journalists tried to calm him down, but he dragged Sasha into a boxroom and called the police. A patrol arrived to nab all the Femen girls on the spot. While the police filled in the paperwork, the guy spat out bile at us, calling us 'cows' and 'painted arseholes'.

Eventually, Sasha was simply sentenced to a fine.

SEX BUSINESS

Initially, we thought we'd carry out just a couple of actions against prostitution. However, they had such an impact that protest against prostitution has become our trademark: 'Ah yes, Femen is the organization that says that Ukraine is not a brothel, and campaigns against sex tourism and prostitution.' In short, the first action resulted in a concerted campaign. For the first time, we started to present a contradictory image, which required some mental effort. We protested against prostitution dressed as prostitutes, thereby unleashing a flood of hatred against us, as if society, and men in particular, insisted on not hearing our message. But our aim was to emphasize that we had the right to wear sexy clothes without running the risk of being mistaken for prostitutes and raped. We wanted to combat the negative image of the Ukrainian woman in the European collective consciousness.

Virtually all our protests in 2009 took place with the slogan 'Ukraine is not a brothel'. One of our most spectacular actions in 2009 was the one we organized during the final of the beauty contest 'Miss Ukraine-Universe 2009'. This glamorous competition was created in 2005 by a former top Ukrainian model Oleksandra Nikolayenko, wife of American billionaire Phil Ruffin who owns casinos in Las Vegas and is Donald Trump's business partner. She is the owner and custodian of the brand name of the contest. The winner then takes part in the 'Miss Universe' competition, jointly run by the aforesaid Donald Trump.

Of course, this is the dream of many young Ukrainian women – to become Miss Ukraine or Miss Universe, and walk in the footsteps of Nikolayenko by marrying a billionaire. It's a particularly unwholesome dream in which the woman immediately views herself as an object, a commodity, and where she's already preparing to play the role of a harem concubine and not a free and fulfilled woman. These competitions with their different stages are a real obstacle course, where the vast majority of girls are sifted out and can eventually become the mistresses of wealthy people or, even worse, prostitutes. The statistics are frightening and show that it's most often the agencies for 'models' that export girls for the sex industry and as luxury escorts.

So we decided to spoil the party: it tramples all over women's dignity. The final was to be held in Mikhaylovskaya Square, at the Intercontinental Hotel. At the entrance lay a red carpet for the upper crust. Our girls, disguised to represent sex slaves, arrived at 3.30 p.m. aboard a luxury car. The 'owners' helped them out of the car and the boot, and rolled out a second red carpet for them. The girls, led by a militant, Galina Sozanskaya, were scantily clad but heavily made-up, wearing 'Miss World'-style crowns and sashes on their chests, with the inscriptions 'Miss Bitch' and 'Vice-Miss Fellatio'. On our red carpet, designed to mock the one used in the contest, they did a few turns parodying the professional women of the sex industry. They chanted: 'Dear model. Don't go into the brothel!' The guards posted around the building cut this action short, after which the girls got back into the car and headed off pronto.

In tandem with this, we demonstrated for four days outside the Rada, to protest against the silence of MPs regarding Bill No. 5223, on criminalizing the clients of the sex industry. We wanted to express our grievances vis-à-vis the Ukrainian state which does nothing to stop this scandal, even though prostitution is officially banned in Ukraine. We carried out propaganda on the Internet to block sites advertising prostitution and sex tourism. The software to block such sites exists and anyone can install it on their computer, but we wanted state intervention. Many foreigners seek information in Internet cafes, and the state could require Ukrainian ISPs to block access to these sites. Unfortunately, the state refused to do so, since some civil servants earn money through prostitution and the state protects them.

The sex industry is one of the biggest illegal businesses. In 2010, the turnover related to prostitution in Ukraine was one and a half billion dollars. And, as these are enormous sums of money, they are controlled by big shots. It's not your ordinary policemen who 'protect' the brothels. Naturally, our initiative couldn't have much effect in a country where the people in power indulge in criminal business. From this point of view, there's no difference between 'Orange' and 'Blue' power.

Let's not forget that we conducted our campaign against prostitution and sex tourism during the presidency of Viktor Yushchenko. This was also the time when we lost our illusions about Yulia Tymoshenko. She was then prime minister, and we turned to her as the head of the government and as a woman. But she didn't see fit to support us or even just respond. We met with total indifference on the part of the government and great indifference on the part of society. Women in Ukraine are so used to being passive victims that they don't want to feel free. They don't know what it is. When a slave is freed, he doesn't know where to go; he's not used to deciding for himself, and this is the most horrible thing in Ukraine: society doesn't know what direction to take.

HOW DID THE IDEA OF GOING TOPLESS COME TO US?

We don't remember exactly how the idea of going topless came about. For quite a long time, we didn't have any definite pattern. Each action included new elements: either a novel concept or a different colour for the banners or other graphic innovations; our way of shouting our slogans; the poses we struck. After each action, we analysed the photos and videos: look, this one worked, we'll adopt it.

We came up with the idea of the crown of flowers by chance. One of the girls brought one along on the day we were in swimsuits for one of our actions. Everyone said: she's crazy, she's come wearing this silly crown on her head. True, in Ukraine, it's not usual to wear an embroidered blouse or a crown of flowers, they're folklore accessories. However, looking at the pictures, we came to the conclusion that the crown had a meaning, and we quickly started to use it, transforming these tiaras into weapons.

During our campaign to block the people accessing pornographic sites, we did a semi-topless protest. We wrote 'Google' on our bare backs, but we stood in a circle, with our backs facing outward, and so our breasts weren't visible, although the media relayed the information that Femen had performed a topless action.

Then we launched the campaign 'Ukrainian time' on the occasion of the inauguration of a big clock of flowers in Kiev. Our slogan was: 'It's no time to be spending money on a clock, while child prostitution is flourishing.' With our bodies, we formed a dial. There was among us a very thin activist, like a little girl. She stuck a band of Scotch tape across her bare chest: she looked more or less topless. The police and the media reacted calmly; it wasn't much commented on.

A few days later, on 24 August 2009, Independence Day in Ukraine, we went out into the street and Oksana volunteered to go really topless. She wore a wreath on her head, her bare chest sported the words 'Ukraine is not a brothel' and she carried a Ukrainian flag. She symbolized the independence and freedom of women. Here again, the police and passers-by didn't react angrily.

Oksana remembers this experience:

For six years, we learnt to be activists. In two years of serious activism, we became more self-confident and more daring, and our organization gained in momentum. There were a good number of girls in our ranks, but we needed a qualitative change that would emphasize that it's women who are protesting, in other words female bodies. By fighting sex tourism in Ukraine, we'd created an image of ourselves as semi-prostitutes, so to speak. We made a provocative use of our bodies. This gradually led us to the idea of carrying out our actions naked. At that time, we weren't well known, we didn't have much money, and nudity was also an allusion to our poverty.

Personally, I've never had misgivings about nudity. I've been on nudist beaches without feeling any discomfort, and I was used to painting nudes. That's how all artists train. The beauty of the female body has always been prized since the days of ancient Greece, and being bold enough to paint it has created artistic revolutions. However, the women in the paintings are objects created by male artists. I wanted to transform my body into a subject. So I decided to conduct an experiment.

On Independence Day 2009, we got everyone together for a photo shoot. I got on to a podium, I took off my top and I started appealing to onlookers to demonstrate in defence of their civil rights and independence, instead of being cajoled by free concerts with stars paid for by the government. It didn't cost me much effort to do this, and I realized that this was our best discovery. It was the maximum simplification of the image of a Femen girl: topless with an inscription on her body and a crown on her head. Simple – and therefore brilliant. There are situations where it's necessary to react immediately, and there's no point in making sets or costumes. It just takes a soldier-girl, a crown and a naked body, and lo and behold, the protest is ready!

Why a crown? It's a Ukrainian symbol. It's worn by unmarried girls; they're free, young and strong. For us, these flowers symbolize freedom and independence. Moreover, when girls adorn their heads this way, it looks pretty, and it's become our hallmark.

At first, the idea of going topless provoked fierce argument. We wondered if it was worth it, if people would like us, if it wasn't sexist behaviour. Inna in particular went through a real crisis of conscience but ended up on side. There was even a time when we wanted to divide Femen into two: the radicals and a more moderate protest group. In fact, 80 percent of girls who were with us in the spring of 2008 left us because of the topless actions and the repression that followed. Another category of activists replaced them. Of the initial nucleus, only the strongest and craziest girls remained. Between the four of us, we arrived at a common denominator, even if each of us has her own vision of Femen.

Our second topless action was very simple but everyone loved it. It was called 'I need a piss!' It was our protest against the lack of public toilets in Kiev. In the city centre, on the Maidan, Oksana went topless, squatted down, lowered her trousers as if she was pissing, and demanded the construction of free public toilets. The police hadn't yet started arresting us, and people responded with a smile – because it's a problem that affects everyone.

In hindsight, we realized that toplessness doesn't cause aggression from the enemy unless it affects masculine interests and isn't a problem when it is used to fight for relatively minor things as far as men are concerned, such as women's issues, prostitution and AIDS. However, once topless actions started to involve politics, the police were ordered to arrest us systematically for 'hooliganism'. There's no law that prohibits women from walking around topless, but the article on hooliganism includes a very vague definition prohibiting 'other actions detrimental to public order'. So we soon got used to the police including toplessness in these 'other actions'. Sometimes, in order to aggravate our case when we were hauled up before the courts, the police also used false witnesses who claimed we swore, spat at passers-by, bit them, etc. They used anything they could to prove that we were hooligans and slap us in jail for a few days.

How did we reach a consensus on going topless? If Oksana was immediately persuaded by the idea, it was a problem for Sasha and Inna, for very different reasons.

Sasha had very personal reasons:

When we were discussing toplessness, the question of me taking part didn't even arise. Let's just say I've got almost nothing to put on display. It's not because I was scared or didn't want to, but I felt it was more for girls with fuller figures. For Oksana, for example, it's perfect, because she has nice breasts.

However, on 2 February 2010, just four days before the second round of the presidential elections, we decided to do a topless action in response to an exhibition at the PinchukArtCentre.[7] One of the paintings being exhibited was by a well-known Ukrainian painter, Sergey Bratkov, with the title *Khortytsia*.[8] The painting shows a reclining Ukrainian woman in embroidered national dress and wearing a crown on her head. Her skirt is raised, and she's not wearing any knickers. Her legs are spread open, and a fly is placed on her private parts. Bratkov created this picture in Sweden where he lives, on and off, and they refused to let this painting cross the border because customs officials decided that this 'work' was pornographic. So Pinchuk exhibited a large photo of the painting.

In our project, I had not only to participate in an action against the exhibition of this picture, which humiliates Ukrainian women, but also to lead two other girls. I thought: *My God, I'll put our whole organization to shame, I have the chest of a boy . . . How awful!* But everything went well. Decked out in dark glasses and crowns, we stripped to our panties, and we sat in front of this painting with our slogans 'Ukraine is not a vagina!' and 'Vaginart'. It was soon over. After ten seconds, the guards grabbed us and led us away. After this episode, which was widely reported in the media, the government commission on morality tried to close down the whole show but then finally gave up.

For Inna, her first topless action was a decisive moment in her inner liberation, but also meant a split with part of her family:

As for going topless, I resisted for a long time. We had endless debates. Anna, Sasha and Oksana were for it, and I was against. There were furious discussions, quarrels, and on several occasions I walked out, slamming the door behind me. I argued that it didn't make sense to protest topless against prostitution; I said that no one would understand us or join us. I now realize that behind these arguments lurked a mental block; I didn't think I was capable of doing it, it was an internal struggle. So as not to jeopardize our group, for a few months we organized topless and non-topless actions. I attended the non-topless actions.

Then we planned an action for Independence Day 2010. At first, we designed it to be partly topless and partly non-topless, so as not to offend me. To everyone's surprise, I said I'd go topless. Then the others said: 'If Inna goes topless, we'll all go topless!' This was the turning point, and after this all our actions became 100 per cent topless.

At first I was scared for a few seconds, but I ordered myself to do it. I removed my T-shirt, and the sky didn't fall on me. What made me decide? The analysis of press reactions. Whatever our message was, if we were dressed in black skirts and white blouses, nobody listened to us. But as soon as one of us came out topless, it caused an uproar and was immediately in the news. This was especially so when we moved on to political protests. So I understood that 'it' worked. Perhaps it's a bit sad that we're forced to strip in order to gain a hearing, but if there's no other way, we need to use toplessness for our own purposes.

So I first removed my T-shirt for Independence Day in Ukraine, 24 August 2010, which I now consider to be my own personal independence day. Since then, I've regularly taken part in topless actions and I have to face the (very violent) reactions of my parents and my whole family. Among my relatives, some said they would kebab me if I went to visit them. In response, I broke off contact with them. It's mainly my maternal family that's the problem. My mother comes from a village near Kherson whose population had been forced to move by Stalin from the Ivano-Frankivsk region, after the occupation of western Ukraine. In this village, we always spoke Ukrainian, we preserved the traditions and every Sunday we would go to church. That's how I was brought up. Every summer, my sister and I were sent to stay with my maternal grandparents, and we spent three months leading cows out to graze in the meadows. I loved it! In this village, they called me 'the divine child' because I was a pretty little girl. Now the divine child has turned into a reviled monster.

So we arrived at the idea of topless actions for rather intuitive reasons. At first glance, it's a superficial symbol of freedom. Girls like to write on their bodies and chant: 'I'm free!' However, if you dig deeper into the reasons why toplessness is so shocking to men, you come down to the economy and the problems of private property.

With the advent of private property, men wanted to transmit this property as an inheritance, and they had to control female sexuality and reproduction. However, when the woman goes out topless to protest, it destroys the very foundation of patriarchy, which is based on the transfer of private property from father to son. It shows that she's freeing herself from the circle drawn by men that limits her sexuality. Her body says: 'I'm naked, I'm free, I'm ready to welcome within myself any man I want.' This makes men mad – the fair sex they can no longer control. Bare breasts make them particularly furious; the breasts are the instrument that nourishes the baby. And now this instrument is going round in complete liberty! If the breast didn't have this nurturing function, there wouldn't be such a fuss about it. The female chest would be perceived in the same way as men's chests. Moreover, by what right does that tool for reproduction, a woman, dare to place on her bare breasts her thoughts, ideas and ideals? What a scandal! For us, it has a deeper meaning: the woman has crossed the borders and the framework set by the male community.

Toplessness covers a whole range of ideas and meanings. It's primarily a way of saying: 'I'm free, I've lost all my hang-ups!' And it's also an incarnation of women protesting; it's Femen. What does our image mean? The crown is the Ukrainian symbol of virginity, and flowers symbolize peaceful protest. The naked body is also a helpless body. You cannot hide a weapon in it. The Ukrainian and foreign police behave stupidly when they viciously attack naked and unarmed women, arrest them, throw them into a van and take them off to prison.

Yes, our protests are over the top. We're the very image of crazy naked women, but we believe that it's just this image that will lead other women in our country and around the world to protest against their condition and demand their rights.

THE NEED FOR SEX EDUCATION

We cannot do the state's job and stop prostitution. Advertising for sexual services is a huge business. If we compare our actions to this industry's turnover, it's not realistic to expect a real result. We wanted to draw the state's attention to this issue but the state doesn't want to intervene; it prefers to get rich from this dirty business. Our campaign did, in spite of everything, allow many people to learn about the existence of this phenomenon.

Unfortunately, Ukrainian women are poor, beautiful and uneducated – they have no choice in the matter! One of the reforms that we demand is education. To begin with, we need to bring in sex education. In our country, the word 'sex' causes helpless laughter among adolescents, that's all. We really must teach feminism, that is, we must give women an awareness of their dignity and their rights. It's the state's job to worry, instead of waiting for society to regenerate itself spontaneously. Perhaps the new generation will understand that we can't go on the way we are now.

In France, when you go into a bookshop, you can see shelves full of feminist literature. In Ukraine, it's unimaginable. People don't even know that such literature exists. Go out into the street in Kiev, not to mention the provinces, and ask: 'What is feminism?' You won't get any answer. It's shameful.

In fact, in addition to education, it's our whole social system that needs to change: we need to restore free higher education,[9] increase wages, open positions up to women, in short, give women the opportunity to live with dignity, instead of turning to prostitution or emigrating. Except that, to do this, we must change the nature of power!

Our society isn't making any progress, and our rulers have an interest in keeping us in this state of backwardness. It's for this reason that Femen takes on a missionary role, even if we adopt an extremist attitude. What we do in the streets is essential. It's necessary to shock people to get them thinking.

6

NO MORE NICE QUIET PROTESTS

When the presidential campaign began in late 2009, Ukraine became polarized between East and West, with supporters of Russia and the Russian language on the one side, and those demanding that Ukrainian be kept as the sole official language and seeking a rapprochement with Europe on the other.[1] All these heated arguments about the future of our country made it clear that we could not talk about women's freedom, the women's revolution, or the emancipation of feminism, if we limited ourselves to purely feminine themes. It would be an illusion to think that prostitution is a separate phenomenon which has nothing to do with the economic and political basis of society. We cannot make women free by solving only some of the problems posed by prostitution or abortion. If women do not participate in the political process, they will never be free. That is why we decided to get involved in political questions, not just social issues. We now had to spice up the major events of politics or economics. We thought this would give us a higher profile and more influence, which would help to advance our ideas and recruit new activists.

'DON'T SELL YOUR VOTES!'

The second round of the presidential election was on 7 February 2010. Ukrainians had to choose between Yanukovych and Tymoshenko. On that day, at about 10 o'clock in the morning, we went to polling station no. 20, located in the building of the Artistic Academy for Children in Kiev. Yanukovych was on the electoral roll here. This was our first political topless action led by Sasha.

Sasha continues:

When we'd previously discussed carrying out a topless action here, I'd been of the opinion that it was a necessity. At that time, I still had a hang-up about my breasts, or rather their absence, but I was chosen as leader. It took me a while to understand that it was the act that counted, and not the size or shape of my breasts.

There were five of us girls accompanied by two young men. We'd designed the following performance: one of the guys had to stand on the shoulders of the other to form a cross with their two bodies and one of the girls, topless, was to be 'crucified'. The press knew that Yanukovych would come to cast his vote at about 11 o'clock and there was a vast media scrum waiting for him. There were maybe three or four hundred television cameras there, in ten rows. On seeing this huge crowd, our guys got scared and ran away. We couldn't do our act with the cross since the said cross had bolted! Meanwhile, the guards sensed that some diversion was being hatched and they tried to block us. I literally tore the panic-stricken girls out of their hands. Today, we know how to push through in such situations, but that day it was a completely new scenario. I ordered the others to strip and unfold our banners. We had several slogans: 'Politicians must not rape the country!', 'We want honest elections!', 'Don't sell your votes!' – but also: 'Today is the day war breaks out'. It was our appeal to common sense, a call on people not to participate in this sham election and to avoid a pointless confrontation between East and West. By that time, we'd already lost our illusions about the 'Orange' regime but that didn't make us support the 'Blues'. In the absence of a viable alternative, the right choice was to vote for 'none of these' so that the elections would not be valid.

Our action indoors lasted only a few seconds, then we rushed outside. It was 17 degrees below zero, and we were practically naked. The police pursued us but they were too fat to run fast enough to catch up with us. We kept going for a few hundred metres, trying to get a car to stop so we could make a getaway. Finally, a vehicle did stop, a man got out and invited us to climb aboard. As soon as the door closed, the man ordered the driver: 'Seryozha, take them to the station!' My God, we'd blithely climbed into an unmarked cop car!

We stayed at the station for a few hours. In fact, the police were happy to welcome the girls of Femen. They offered us bread and bacon[2] and all the meals their wives had prepared, and they served us tea. The atmosphere was cheerful; the cops kept making jokes. They were not really against us, but they'd been given orders to arrest everyone who wasn't registered to be present for Yanukovych's arrival. So we ate well at the station, and we quietly returned home after paying a small fine. Despite the fact it was quite gentle, this first arrest marked the beginning of our persecution.

This first political topless action was a turning point in the life of our organization. We suddenly left a naive world to find ourselves at a very different level – now we were playing with the big boys, the 'godfathers' of politics. This provoked an immediate opposition from them. They told us things like: 'Why are you interfering in all this, girls? Do you really need to? You look after your prostitutes and stop sticking your noses into our business.' The secret services and the police began to watch us closely.

Previously, we'd been in the habit of informing the city hall of our actions in advance. We sent a letter, and also called the municipal security department so they'd send a few people to the site to protect us against potential crazies. But after our action at the polling booth, they nabbed us as soon as we tried to strip. So we started to behave like 'partisans' and carry out our actions without warning.

THE MINISTER FOR WASHING UP

On 17 March 2010, we decided to organize an action against the lack of women in the new government formed by Yanukovych's prime minister, Mykola Azarov. Out of the thirty or so cabinet members, not one was a woman! In addition, Azarov had the insolence to justify this total absence by stating that a woman wasn't able to say 'no' firmly.

Our plan was as follows: dozens of Femen girls would head to the main entrance of the building of the Cabinet of Ministers (Kabmin for short) dressed in men's suits. There, we would take off these suits and, in really sexy clothes, dash to the government meeting room. We prepared briefcases on which was written: 'Minister for Dirty Socks', 'Minister for Borscht', 'Minister for Washing Up', 'Minister for Sweeping', etc. These were, of course, ministries that we'd invented!

We didn't manage to carry this plan out. As we approached the Kabmin, we found our access to the building blocked by a police cordon. Let's hear Inna relate the sequence of events and the way they impacted on her life:

> Suddenly, I saw a way through and I ran towards the entrance. Just then, a police car arrived, apparently intending to stop us. I then started to unbutton my pair of men's trousers to turn into a woman. I didn't have the slightest intention of stripping completely, I'd never have even imagined such a thing in my worst nightmares. I tried to remove my trousers just to show that I was a woman and was wearing women's clothes under my man's suit. But no sooner had I opened my flies than I was arrested. In the news, several media reported that one Femen activist had been about to strip completely outside the Kabmin. After this story, we began to be associated with naked protests.
>
> While I was being dragged off to the van, I kept on yelling. I needed to kick up the biggest fuss while I still could! It was my first arrest, I didn't know what to expect. I'll admit that I was very scared. Not only because of the uncertainty about what would happen at the station, but because of the mere fact of being arrested. I was a college student, I worked at the city hall, and Mom might go off the trolley if she saw me appearing on the news, given the circumstances.
>
> In fact, I spent only two hours at the station. There was a very nice policeman who poured me endless cups of tea. This deputy director of the Pechersky station became a friend. When we get arrested, he always takes a humane attitude towards us and brings us tea in our cells. If he's given the order to keep us there for twenty-four hours, he obeys, but he behaves in a very fatherly way and doesn't treat us like prostitutes. That's already a great deal!
>
> Finally, I paid a token fine and next day I went to work as usual. The minute I arrived, the head of the press service at the city hall, where I'd worked for a year, asked me into

her office. She set down in front of me a stack of photos of our action outside the Kabmin and told me: 'You can't work here any more.' She didn't say anything else. I realized there was no point arguing, I took my things and I left. Once I was outside, I started to cry.

My parents had been so proud that at the age of nineteen I was working in the city hall and could earn a living in Kiev ... Now, I didn't know where to go or what to do. I called Anna and I told her I'd just been fired. She responded simply: 'Too bad, but don't forget that we're right behind you!'

I was both furious that I was treated so badly at the city hall, and happy I didn't have to do that filthy job any more. I'd had enough of writing stuff singing the praises of Mayor Chernovetskyi and his team, all equally corrupt and incompetent. I'd loathed the job from the beginning but my parents had pressured me: 'How can you say that? It's such a prestigious job! At your age! You need to swallow your pride and get on with it. That's how everyone lives.' It's true that, in our country, that's how everyone lives, but this was no reason for me to swallow my pride. Fate had helped me to get rid of a heavy burden; I knew for a fact that it was barely possible to be an honest journalist in Ukraine.

I then decided not to look for another job but to devote myself entirely to fighting on behalf of Femen. As I could no longer pay my rent, I moved into a student hostel. I was put in a tiny room where there were two bunk beds and one ordinary bed. There were five of us in a few square metres. I started work full time, but completely unpaid, for Femen.

It was a period of terrible rows with my parents. Mom was in hysterics; she was crying constantly. She didn't speak to me for two months. My father threatened to bring me home to Kherson by force. Finally, I decided that it was time to switch roles. Previously, it was my parents who had raised me, but now it was my turn to take care of their education. During our conversations over the phone, I explained that I wasn't giving up my activities and their criticisms were only strengthening my decisions.

Eventually, we stopped quarrelling. My parents even continued to help me a little. They knew that, at least, I was still studying. So they still hoped they'd be able to 'get me back on the right path'. However, their financial aid was, to say the least, modest, and some days, I didn't have enough to pay for a metro ticket and came home from college on foot, even in the winter. It was hard, but I thought: 'You've made your choice! Forward march!' Sometimes guys from college took me home by car. Not very feminist, you'll say.

DEMOCRATIC BITCHES

In 2010, there was an event that convinced us that the time for 'nice, quiet' protests was gone forever. With the coming to power of Yanukovych, the atmosphere quickly became more repressive. Officers of the Ukrainian Security Service (SBU) started to pay visits to Femen activists who were students. They hauled the girls up before the dean of their faculty and subjected them to interrogations. 'What is Femen? Who's your leader? Where does your funding come from?' In fact, they already knew the answers because we had no secrets; it was just a way of putting pressure on the girls and intimidating them.

We decided to organize a protest action – 'Hey you mutts, hands off!' – just outside the SBU building. We dreamt up a very hard-core performance; we'd be playing the role of 'democratic bitches'. We officially informed the city hall of the date of the event, on 23 June 2010. The night before the demonstration, there was a ring at Anna's doorbell: 'Hello, we're from the SBU.'

Anna would never have imagined these people could behave in this way.

'Are you ready to talk to us?'

'Sure, why not?'

She continues her story:

I thought they'd go home, but one of them (there were two) grabbed me by the neck and pushed me into the lift. Downstairs, they made me get into a car parked in front of my building.

'Tomorrow, you cancel the protest!'

'How? Sixty journalists have already told me they're definitely attending. However do you think I'm going to tell them not to come, just because you're threatening me?'

It was your classic scenario: one of them played good cop, and the other bad cop.

The first was very rude; he growled at me: 'Cut the crap!'

And the second whispered: 'Anna, calm down and think. We're just giving you a little word of advice. You can cancel the demo and say it's because of some technical problem.'

This session in the car lasted three hours. I realized that the situation was serious. They went on to make direct threats, such as: 'If you don't cancel this action tomorrow, A and B and C . . . [it was a long list of girls] won't even be able to set a foot outside. They'll be arrested on the spot.' I was getting more and more scared, and I was torn up inside. What should I do? If I accepted, it meant the end of our movement because they'd have carried on putting pressure on us every time. I had to find a way out.

Finally, I told the guys that I'd cancel the action. What other choice did I have? From the car, I called the protest coordinator, Tatiana, and told her that the action wouldn't be happening, without giving any other details. I phoned her again when I returned home, and I fixed an emergency

meeting at dawn with Sasha, Inna, Tatiana and Jenia. I told
the girls what had happened.

It became clear to us that with the coming to power of
Yanukovych, a new era had begun, and that we'd now be
living in a different state, with different objectives and rules
of the game. We couldn't play that game. We were now
under the thumb of the police services!

How could we preserve the movement? How could we
resist giving in and losing momentum, while still remaining free and alive? I realized that the lives of each of us
depended on our decision. So I suggested that we shouldn't
carry out the action itself, but neither should we cancel the
rendezvous with the journalists: that way we could inform
them of what had happened and tell them we were under
strong pressure from the special services. I was convinced
that this publicity would save us (the Ukrainian press
was still relatively free) and would prevent the SBU from
attacking us. We needed to play our trump card. Perhaps
the cops would leave us alone?

That day was Inna's twentieth birthday. I felt particularly responsible for her; she was the youngest among us.
However, we needed to take – together – a decision that
would define our lives for years to come. Risk or no risk.
There was also an element of ego in all this, with the sub-
text: 'Oh, you bastards, we won't allow you to treat us like
that.' Finally, we decided to tell the press everything, and
this worked.

This decision gave us strength and courage. But it marked
the beginning of our open war with the Ukrainian government, a war which continues. The persistent refusal of
official bodies to register our movement, our relationship
with the SBU, the courts, the president and the patriarch:
none of this is simple. Yanukovych hates 'those crazy girls'

as he calls us. This is great, because that's exactly the effect we were after: let the misogynists and the dictators hate us!

FEMEN AGAINST PUTIN

Once Yanukovych had come to power, relations between Russia and Ukraine started to improve. At the same time, the atmosphere in the country has become unbearable. In May 2010, we protested against the visit of President Medvedev. It was a performance that we called 'Lacerated by a bear'.[3] On the body of one of our activists, we drew the bloody traces of bear's claws. She stripped in front of the main entrance of the Yanukovych administration. The symbol was unequivocal: we didn't want to feed our country and Ukrainian women to the Russian bear. Anna put it well in her press release: 'The rapprochement between Ukraine and Russia represents a threat to the interests of Ukrainian women who are only just beginning to feel like free European women. For them, freedom smells like French perfume, and not like the boots of a Russian soldier.'

But we kept a more important protest for the true master of Russia, Vladimir Putin. When he came to visit Ukraine on 28 October 2010, as prime minister, we organized an action near a statue of Lenin in the city centre. In the cold, under a heavy downpour, we came out with eloquent placards proclaiming: 'Ukraine is not Alina', 'You're not going to fuck us!' and 'We're not giving ourselves to gnomes from the Kremlin!' We wanted to protest against the insolent intrusion of Putin's Russia in the political, economic and cultural arena of Ukraine. Yanukovych had been in power for only ten months, but we could already see that each of 'Big Brother's' trips to Ukraine was followed by a narrowing of the freedom of speech and protest, as in Russia.

The slogan 'Ukraine is not Alina' referred to the alleged

connection between Putin and Alina Kabaeva, the gymnast who had become a member of the Duma, who gave birth to a boy named Dima, in honour of President Dmitry Medvedev. To emphasize this point, some of us were carrying baby dolls. We wanted Putin to understand that he could have all the mistresses he wanted and give them kids, but the 'gnome' – he's very short – had no right to 'fuck' Ukraine or try to seize its wealth. This action was really the opening skirmish in our fight against the dictatorship.

This time, we weren't arrested. Since we hadn't informed the city hall about our action, there were no police near the monument. We'd simply alerted foreign journalists as we were sure they wouldn't give the game away. So we carried out our action, then we scarpered. Four hours later, a group of police officers showed up at the Cupid Cafe, our headquarters at the time. They tried to arrest us, but we sat on the floor with our arms linked, holding tight to each together. That day, they left empty-handed but then they came back every day. We considered that we'd committed no crime. At worst, the only thing they were entitled to do was fine us. This persecution was totally illegal. So we decided to protest publicly.

A week later, we went to the main entrance of the police department HQ. We stripped, keeping on our briefs with large stripes like those on prisoners' clothes. We put our hands up as if we wanted to surrender. This time, the police didn't waste any time. The cops immediately dragged us off to a van and took us to the station to sign the papers, and then to the court. By order of the chief of police, the judge sentenced Inna and Sasha, but not the other girls, to twenty-four hours in prison for 'hooliganism'. Sasha remembers this experience and her parents' reaction:

> This was the first time in jail for both of us. We were very scared, even if we were only spending one night there.

Above all, we didn't know how to break the news to our parents. What if it killed our mothers? We stayed at the station until midnight, when the police gave us something to eat and even tried to take our minds off things. Compared to their regular customers, we were rare birds.

We witnessed one horrible scene. A ten-year-old girl called to say that her father was drunk and chasing after her mother with a knife in his hand. The duty officer replied, without hesitation, that she should just calm her father down herself, as the police didn't deal with drunks. She phoned back some minutes later saying, 'My father's going to kill my mother, please just come!' An hour later, the police finally decided to go along and brought back the father, dead drunk, and the mother and daughter. The father was deaf and dumb, and as they didn't know what to do with him, they decided to release him. The girl begged them to keep him in the station until he sobered up, because this would calm him down for the next few days. They explained that they could only arrest him if he killed or hurt someone. We found this logic incredible. It meant the police couldn't keep a drunkard who was threatening to kill his wife, but could keep two girls like us for twenty-four hours, just for a mere protest.

Then we were placed in two separate cells on different sides of the corridor, so we couldn't communicate by tapping on the wall. Anyway, we were too scared to think about that. When you're locked in a small cell, it makes you claustrophobic. The windows were covered with white paint, so we couldn't see what was happening outside. We just knew when it was daytime or night-time. I was so tired that I slept like a log. In the morning, my first thought was: *Mom is probably already dead.*

Of course, Mom was furious. As a little girl, I'd never had any conflict with my parents. The quarrels started when I began a correspondence course and I left Khmelnytskyi for Kiev. I came to my parents' for Christmas Eve 2009, and my father locked me up. He tore up my return ticket and confiscated my coat, my keys and my mobile, so I couldn't escape. This horrible situation lasted several days, with cries and tears. We even almost came to blows.

Finally, my parents had let me go, but a few months later, something weird happened. Two men phoned Anna and our friend Viktor saying that if I didn't return pronto to Khmelnytskyi, they'd kill me and murder them. It was absurd, and we didn't know how to react. I called my parents, who claimed that someone had tried to force their door. They claimed they were being chased by dangerous people who'd already caused my father's car to break down, and this had nearly cost him his life. Something told me this was just being staged by my parents, but as Anna and Viktor found themselves involved, I decided to get to the bottom of it.

Without telling anyone, I went to Khmelnytskyi and I called my parents. They suggested that I go and see them at home, but I refused because I was scared they'd lock me up again. We agreed to meet in a cafe. When they began, tears in their eyes, telling me about the threats and pressures they were suffering from unknown people, I told them to make a complaint. They gave the game away when they refused to do so. So I went back to Kiev. We didn't have any more contact for several months.

Then we were reconciled, but they're still not always able to accept what I do. Sometimes Dad gives me a discreet wink, but my mother refuses to calm down. She keeps asking me: 'When are you going to get married and have children? All the girls your age are already married, and you're still single. Can't you see you're already old?' I'm only twenty-four, and I don't feel old at all!

AGAINST STONING

In November 2010, we carried out two actions in support of Sakineh Mohammadi Ashtiani, sentenced by the Iranian mullahs to stoning, for adultery and complicity in the murder of her husband. We supported her because we believe that feminism knows no borders. We have chosen to defend the rights of women in all places. In Iran, the treatment suffered by women is despicable. How can we tolerate this?

In fact, we first put feminism into practice, then we consider the theoretical framework of our actions. This was the case for our first topless protest. We decided to do this because it was radical and this 'pop feminism' could attract the media, but it was only two years later that we began to theorize about the cultural, political and anthropological contexts to which our naked bodies could lend themselves.

At the time when we were discussing the theme 'All men are bastards', it was clear to us that it was the lack of female solidarity that made it difficult to practise feminism. In fact, women behave most of the time like competitors rather than allies. We rebelled against this approach. We are in solidarity with all women, regardless of their country of origin, their age or the colour of their skin.

Sakineh's case was particularly scandalous. At the time of our actions, this mother of two children had already been in prison for five years, and her confession had been obtained under torture, irrespective of the fact that, as an Azeri, she spoke no Persian. She was to suffer stoning, a medieval punishment of unspeakable cruelty.

It was the Iranian Embassy in Kiev that we decided to attack. For once, we were fully dressed. On 3 November 2010, we organized a picket near the embassy. We yelled: 'Assassins, leave Ukraine!', 'Stone Age in Iran!', and we threw stones at the walls of the embassy. We wanted the ambassador to come out to talk to us, but he refused. Surprisingly, no one arrested us. We 'reoffended' a week later. We burst into the opening ceremony for the Festival of Iranian Culture in Ukraine, in the centre of Kiev. Our girls were topless, with crowns on their heads and ropes knotted around their necks, and they bore the slogans 'Do not kill your women!' and 'Down with the murderous regime!' The ambassador's bodyguards neutralized us, of course, and threw us out, but the ceremony was interrupted and the ambassador, who had just started his speech, withdrew rather quickly.

Through these actions, we wanted to encourage the civilized world to boycott countries that practise barbaric Islamic traditions. We also called on the Ukrainian authorities to break off all relationships with Iran. For us, it was an outrage that a Festival of Iranian Culture could be organized in Ukraine when the Iranian 'justice' decision was causing a worldwide scandal. Her stoning was reported only under the pressure of international public opinion.

Our actions in support of Sakineh were noted in Iran, despite the censorship imposed by the mullahs. We don't know if we were any help to this woman who, like her lawyer, is still languishing in prison. In any case, we have received many calls and emails from Iranians. They wrote: 'You are so far away and have no particular link with Iran. Ukraine has no economic or financial interests in Iran, but you took action to support us, and we thank you.' Too bad we've never received any thanks from the Russians for our fight against the autocratic misogynist known as Putin!

'IT'S FOR SWEETS'

The more we intensified our activities, the more we needed a place where we could meet from time to time, and that could be our headquarters. At the end of 2009, we finally found a refuge at the Cupid cafe-bar in Pushkin Street, parallel to Khreshchatyk Avenue. This is a trendy place where intellectuals hang out and where you can meet interesting people. One day, we arranged an appointment with the correspondent of a French radio station in this cafe. Fyodor Balandin, the owner, approached us after the interview and asked us: 'Are you those crazy girls who protest topless? I love you. Do you have a place to do your work? Otherwise, you can set up here.'

Fyodor knew that we couldn't pay, and he didn't require us to order drinks. He still gave us a table where we could spend days and nights, and the bar stayed open until the early morning. We were even offered cups of tea! We stayed two years at the Cupid, and many of our ideas were born there. We also used it as a place to change before actions, instead of squatting in the lobbies of apartment blocks. It wasn't until the middle of 2012 that we finally had enough resources to rent an office.

Since we started out, and even now, we've been lucky enough to get outside help, which is very valuable to us. We have photographers and cameramen who photograph and film us, designers who help us plan our actions, and all this for free. For example, our photographer Yaroslav Debelyi has been with us since 2008. He accompanies us at our actions, even when they're very dangerous. When he helps us, he sometimes takes unpaid leave from his job.

To begin with, our expenses were ridiculously small, but then life started to become more complicated. As soon as one of us was seen protesting topless, she was fired the very next day. It was then that we gained our first sponsors, Jed Sunden, a Ukrainian media mogul of American origin, who lives in Kiev, and Helmut Joseph Geier, a famous composer of techno and hip-hop, known as DJ Hell, who lives in Munich. These are people who had nothing to do with politics but who were bowled over by our movement, and did not seek to dictate their conditions or control the actions.

However, when we became more radical, we had a major disagreement with Jed Sunden. He was convinced that we should focus only on feminine subjects, namely, prostitution and sex tourism. Despite this split, we're still grateful to him because he was the first to support us. He helped us out with small amounts: one hundred dollars and then two hundred dollars per month. It was his moral support that we found especially valuable because he's a famous man in the world of the press. It was he who paid for our domain name, femen. org.

As for Geier, he even participated in two of our actions, where he played the role of a sex tourist. He also did a great deal to popularize our movement, thanks to his own high profile. He thinks that our protests are exceptional and unique forms of the struggle against female prostitution. Thousands of young Ukrainian women are 'exported' under false pretexts to Germany, where pimps shut them up in brothels. As a German, he is revolted by these practices.

We suggested to our first donors that they should form a board of patrons. Admittedly, it was a matter of very small amounts, but at the time, this assistance was vital. The years 2010 and 2011 were tough. At one point, we had an average budget of 2,000 hryvni per month, which corresponds to just over 200 dollars. Almost all of this money was used to pay our rent. With the rest, we bought the paint, paper for placards and banners, artificial flowers for our crowns. And we ate very little . . .

Then a friend, Taras, gave us the incredible amount of 1,000 dollars, which allowed us to invest in our own merchandising. At first we didn't know how to sell our products. We had a large number of T-shirts printed, and cups and calendars made, which remained in stock for three months. We even walked through the streets trying to offer our calendars to passers-by, but people preferred to take pictures with us rather than to buy our 'souvenirs'. We had to learn our business know-how on the Internet, and today our e-shop works pretty well. With the growing popularity of the movement, we could develop our brand and now we sell our products to fans all over the planet.

It's also thanks to the Internet that gifts are deposited in our account, but we sometimes receive gifts 'in kind'. Most often it's small symbolic donations, like a big box of chocolates sent from Belarus or a teapot given to Sasha by someone who had seen her using an empty jam jar to brew her tea in. For a long time, an anonymous donor sent us 2–3,000 roubles per month, accompanying his gifts with a laconic note: 'This is for sweets.'

We should also mention Artemy Lebedev, the founder and director of the most famous and most expensive design workshop in the whole post-Soviet world; generally, only the big companies can call on his services. He created our logo: two circles, one yellow and one blue, separated by a vertical line, which reproduces the Cyrillic letter Ф (F), and also symbolizes the Ukrainian flag. Below is the signature 'Femen'. This logo has a universal potential, as you simply need to change the colours to fit any country. Lebedev did this work for us for free because he felt that we had a future. He says: 'This logo is also a symbol of Ukraine, breasts, cheerfulness, and opposition: it's the sting of a wasp.' A good point: it's really all of these at once.

OKSANA MOVES TO KIEV

Oksana was the last to join us in Kiev permanently, in early 2011. Until then, she'd tried to combine her activities as an artist and icon painter with her life as a feminist:

For two years, I shuttled between Kiev and Khmelnytskyi, with two weeks in each. Before I settled there, I took part in an unusual art project. I have a friend, Andrei, a contractor who has managed to raise rather a lot of money. Today, he has two hobbies: he hitch-hikes around the world with his backpack, and supports artistic projects. In 2010, he chose ten young artists, including me, and he sent us to Egypt, at his own expense. He rented a villa on the Red Sea where we could create without any financial worries. We drew, wrote and made videos, but in early 2011, the revolution broke out and we were forced to pack up. It had become too dangerous. Unfortunately, the works that I created in Egypt were burned in Khmelnytskyi, in the fire at my parents. It was in Egypt that I took the decision to devote myself entirely to Femen. The distance allowed me to realize how much I was missing Femen activities.

Life in Kiev wasn't easy. Sasha first rented a room with four other girls but then she had to rent a three-bedroom flat with seven girls as flatmates. I could never bear all the noise and the fuss! Inna and Anna rented a room each. When I arrived in Kiev, I also rented a room in a communal apartment. I was unlucky as my neighbours were very unpleasant people, but that didn't matter – I'm used to adversity.

A POP FEMINISM

When we plan our actions and, more generally, think about how we want to develop our strategy, we think about two aspects. We view ourselves as 50 per cent feminist organization, and 50 per cent group actionists.[4] Each time, we aim to create an action that is unprecedented, both its content and its form. You might say that sometimes, for us, form comes first.

However, are we an artistic group? On this subject, opinions differ. Inna doesn't dispute the artistic dimension of the group, but she defines Femen rather as a subversive mixture of politics, sex, scandal, assault and art that could be called pop feminism. Of course, the boundary between art and actionism is blurred, and contemporary artists who deal with social issues in their works are thick on the ground, such as the Russian group Voina.[5]

Inna explains:

> We create costumes, we sing, we put on sketches, and set up installations. Oksana is an artist and she also works with us. However, if we position ourselves as artists, this will lower our level of aggressiveness. For example, Pussy Riot presented themselves as punk artists and suddenly, they do indeed seem less radical to Western eyes, although this hasn't helped them avoid jail in Russia.

Inna insists:

> When you're dealing with 'art', it smoothes out all the rough angles of an action. But we want to be perceived as dangerous by our enemies. We are a radical feminist group. We state this loud and clear, we are activists and we protest as citizens. Yes, I'm a radical activist; I'm able to take a power saw and cut down a cross, and I don't do so as an artist but because I'm protesting as a citizen. Thus we can fight on equal terms against misogyny, power, the Church, dictatorship.

Anna summarizes the debate by siding more with Inna:

> Art is everywhere. If you can do something well, for me, that thing is art. I'm a woman of the left, and I consider that

a good carpenter is more of an artist than a painter who smears a canvas. Naturally, there are artistic elements in our business. Some people in artistic circles perceive it as an artistic expression, while those from a political background see more of its political aspects. In the past, we had a higher proportion of art as we tried to associate gaudy forms with non-radical actions, playing on the contrast.

We use artistic elements to serve radical political protest, and it's in this sense that we're interesting. We've given up on dull, unimaginative protests. It was our appearance that revived both the political and the artistic scenes. We have forced others to behave in other ways, instead of taking to the streets with flags, as did our great-grandfathers.

Finally, Oksana underlines her viewpoint and signs off:

We live in a society where the entertainment industry is dominant. Consumers are very demanding, and we're forced to take into account their desires and ability to assimilate information. If we want to be heard, we must create short actions that strike the imagination, dramatized performances with a clear, concise message. They should excite the masses, bring them to the boil, because that's how we can change things.

Are we creating art? One year ago, we were still having quite a few arguments over this. The girls accused me of having said in an interview that we were artists. I defended my point of view. I think that true artists – I'm not talking of artisans daubing canvases and then selling them as merchandise – are not passive figures. The main task of art is revolution. We call for a revolution: one person will use music, another painting, another her own body. An artist is always a revolutionary. I hope this is true in my case.

7

FEMEN GOES ALL OUT

'GREG, OVER HERE!'

In February 2011, the New Zealand FM radio channel Rock FM launched an extravagant contest, with the slogan 'Win a wife!' The winner's prize was a flight to Ukraine and twelve nights' hotel accommodation on site. As for the possibilities of finding a wife, the winner was supposed to choose from among the female clients of a dating agency that was co-sponsoring this contest. On 28 February, the radio announced the name of the 'lucky winner', a winemaker, Greg, 'the handsomest and gentlest single guy in New Zealand'.

This case caused a scandal in New Zealand, especially in the small local Ukrainian community and among Facebook users. However, the female director of the radio station defended the competition, saying that it was 'all for fun' and that nobody was being forced to marry or settle in New Zealand.

We started a campaign against this shameful competition.

The truth is that Greg was being offered a free sex tour, in which he would have to choose himself a wife, just as a concubine is chosen in a slave market. This campaign had its effect and the New Zealand radio announced that Greg, now guilty about his ill-starred fame, had decided not to take up his prize. We suspected a trick.

So we researched all the possible ways of travelling to Ukraine from New Zealand on the date announced. Apparently, the most convenient itinerary for him was to come to Donetsk, with a stopover in Moscow. So Inna went to see if she could recognize him from among all the passengers arriving from Moscow. We gave this action the name: 'Here, not even a mouse will pass unnoticed.' Inna was wearing black skinny jeans and an unbuttoned jacket, and her breasts were partly covered by two photos of Greg that she had stuck to her nipples. It was a little ruse, so that she wouldn't be locked up straightaway. She also held up a sign like those used to greet travellers: it read, 'Greg, over here!' Inna was accompanied by a local activist, Aleksandra Nemchinova, who wasn't up to baring her breasts but held up a sign saying: 'Ukraine is not a brothel'. As it was not a political action, police and staff at the airport mainly responded with a smile, apart from a grumpy customs official who pointedly asked the girls for their identity papers. Finally, Greg didn't come. He'd kept his word.

In our struggle for a more civilized image of Ukraine, it was a small victory.

THE ONSLAUGHT ON EURO 2012

When Ukraine was elected to host the finals of the European Football Championship, Euro 2012, we leapt into action. The four new stadiums were hastily built: as they were poorly designed, they did not meet modern requirements. But they

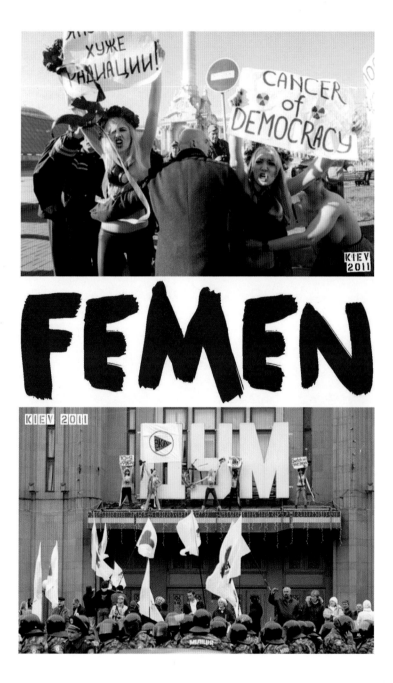

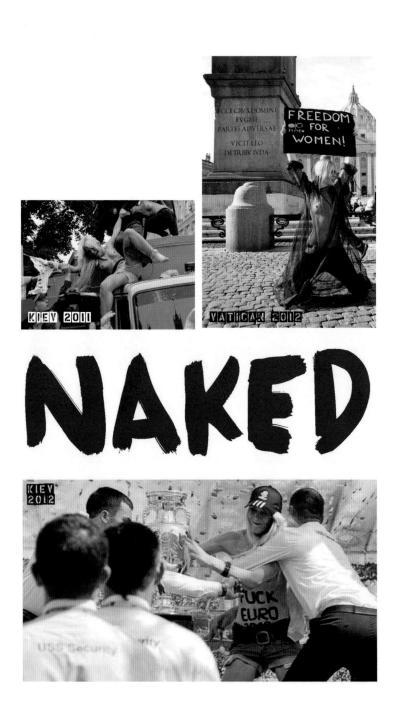

KIEV 2011

FREE WOMAN

ROME 2011

The 42nd annual meeting of the World Economic Forum Davos 2012

SEXTREMISM

KIEV 2009

RIOT

were a financial drain on the economy of Ukraine, as the money invested by the government went to construction companies which, in exchange for juicy contracts, offered a generous discount to the officials involved. The usual system! As for the arrival of fans from around the world, you might have expected ugly consequences: men swallowing industrial quantities of beer during and after games, and then going off to find a prostitute for the night. In short: football-beer-fuck. Not to mention the risk of spreading AIDS and tuberculosis.

Officials tried to reassure public opinion. According to them, there was no link between the championship and sex tourism. They were wrong, of course. A few months before the championship, a fan from Manchester went to Ukraine to inform his club of the state of preparations. Upon his return, he put a video on YouTube commenting on what had most surprised him. He spoke of the thousands of offers of a 'massage' which he found on his arrival at the airport, where he was also handed a tourist map of the city centre distributed by the Office of Tourism, where addresses were given for 'escort' services, with photos. This story was confirmed by many other tourists. We therefore contacted the Ukrainian authorities, demanding an information campaign against sex tourism, and requesting the criminalization of clients of the sex industry. As on previous occasions, it was met with a blunt refusal.

We organized a series of protests against the transformation of Ukraine into *Whoreland*. On 29 October 2011, a great ceremony was planned in Lviv to celebrate the opening of the fourth stadium. The programme included a spectacular laser show and a performance with 2,000 actors relating the eventful history of the capital of western Ukraine. The construction was unfinished: there were still three cranes in front of the stage, and piles of rubble and sand, but this didn't matter – the show must go on! This was the parade we decided to rain on. We arrived at the VIP entrance of the stadium. We had inscriptions reading 'Fucking Euro' on our breasts and began to smash crockery at the entrance, while chanting: 'Ukraine's gonna lose!' Of course, this wasn't meant as a prediction of the championship results, but of the damage done to our country.

'STOP THIS CIRCUS'

In May 2011, the Europe Days were celebrated in Kiev, an opportunity for the political nobs to parade. On 21 May, the Minister of Foreign Affairs in Ukraine (Konstantin Grishchenko), the mayor of Kiev (Aleksandr Popov), and ambassadors of European countries gathered at the official opening ceremony with the usual pompous verbiage, of the kind: 'Today, we see that Europe is beating in the heart of Ukraine.' Thus spoke Grishchenko. All of these ceremonies would, of course, never replace the difficult realities of the European integration of the country. For example: while Yushchenko unilaterally abolished visas for Europeans, Ukrainians still have to struggle to get a European visa. They must make an appointment at the consulate of the relevant country well in advance, gather a pile of documents, show their bank statements, etc., and they still can't be sure of the result. This particularly affects young women, who are always perceived as future prostitutes.

On our side, we called on EU officials to abolish visas for Ukrainians and recognize that Ukraine is a European country, with all the practical consequences this entails. We need European standards in politics, a higher standard of living to 'catch up' with Europe, and equality between men and women – what we *don't* need is this ridiculous circus, with these empty words, and these endless balloons being released.

We prepared an action that was carried out by two of our

activists, Valentina Chebotko and Eva Litvak. Topless, and wearing red clown noses, they managed to break through the security checkpoint and rushed up to the mayor, yelling 'Stop this circus!'

The cops seized them and dragged them to the ground, before shoving them into a police van, in front of foreign journalists, who were very perturbed by this scene. It was really not very 'European'! After two days in protective custody, our two comrades were sentenced by the District Court to five days' imprisonment, which was unheard of at the time. The hardening of the regime's stance was visible to all. That wasn't the end of the matter. Sasha tells us what happened next:

> Two days later, while the girls were still in jail, cops came round to ring and knock on my door. I saw from my window that a patrol car was parked near my building. 'We just want to talk to you,' they said through my door. It was 7 a.m. but I immediately called my lawyer. He advised not to open to them because they didn't have an arrest warrant or search warrant. They waited two hours before leaving, and I fled from the house. In the morning, they carried out the same scenario with our activist Jenia Kraizman. It was open season.
>
> We decided to react. On the one hand, we issued a press release where we said: 'The members of the Femen movement fear for their lives, their health and their freedom. We ask the public not to believe in the Public Prosecutor and the justice system, if they say they have searched our homes and found weapons, drugs, pornographic publications, stolen bras or even maps of the underground communications networks in Rada and Kabmin in preparation for an attack.' This is a very common practice in the SBU and its 'big brother', the FSB, which is used to imprison

troublemakers. However, we had our little revenge. Outside the city hall, myself and Inna showed our buttocks on which was written the word 'arse',[1] while holding up a sign that said 'For Popov'. Of course, we were wearing G-strings, but this was still our way of giving the finger to the mayor, before scarpering.

On 28 May, we welcomed Eva and Valentina as they emerged from prison. We congratulated them and we drank champagne. Our conclusion? We told ourselves that, from now on, we'd act even more boldly and run even faster.

DOWN WITH CENSORSHIP! DOWN WITH THE POLICE STATE!

On 1 April 2011, the Ukrainian Internet Governance Forum opened its doors in the International Exhibitions Park, on the left bank in Kiev. There was talk of business, advertising, social networks and Internet technologies. Nearly 3,000 participants had registered. However, we had accounts to settle with the Ukrainian ISPs and the authorities. Indeed, shortly before the event, our accounts and the different pages of Femen on various social networks had been blocked. ISPs had tried to impose their patriarchal stereotypes on the whole Internet community. Meanwhile, the Russian censorship had blocked access to an article about us published on the site of the Russian opposition radio station, Echo of Moscow. Sasha, who has the gift of the gab, accused our censors of 'indiscriminate breastophobia'. In any case, it was clearly both political and sexist censorship. So we decided to perform an action at the opening of the forum.

As usual, we based our action around a set of words. In English, blocking is sometimes called a 'ban', and in Russian this is a homonym of the word for 'bathhouses', with a slightly different pronunciation. During the opening speech, the four of us burst into the exhibition hall. We were topless, wearing bathing caps with long ribbons attached and thin birch branches – traditionally used in our bathhouses for whipping ourselves so as to accelerate blood circulation. We had signs: 'Internet without censorship', and we yelled, 'Your fucking bathhouses are suffocating us!' Without wasting time, we jumped on to the stage and whipped the rapporteur and the members of the presidium, before tackling the front rows of the public. This led to a joyful chaos that the press did not fail to report!

WHEN IT GETS ON OUR TITS

Our actions against Euro 2012 were repeatedly put down. On our side, we had no intention of dropping our fight. Following our action at the entrance of the Olimpiyskiy Stadium in Kiev, on 28 September 2011, with our slogan 'Euro 2012 without prostitution!', our activists were arrested and then sentenced by the District Administrative Court of Pechersky. To protest against this arrest, which violated the right of citizens to protest peacefully, we designed a pretty spectacular performance. Our slogan was full-on: 'It's a dog's life that gets on our tits.'

To illustrate this, Oksana made some bras and muzzles with lengths of iron wire that she twisted in places, with a great deal of care, to mimic barbed wire. After all, we didn't want to get hurt by this outfit! Decked in these attributes, reminiscent of instruments of torture, our girls went to demonstrate outside the court. Inna, with a crown of red peonies, was particularly impressive. Our activists managed to break the police cordon round the court, shouting: 'Nobody will gag us, nobody will muzzle our tits!', and, more simply, 'Shame!' It should be noted that this was when we had a real confrontation with supporters of Yulia Tymoshenko, whose trial was happening at the same time, in the same court.

BUT WHO IS YULIA TYMOSHENKO?

During the trial of the former prime minister of Ukraine, Yulia Tymoshenko, in summer and autumn 2011,[2] camps formed outside the courtroom, with Yulia's supporters on the one hand and Yanukovych's on the other. The former were requesting the unconditional release of Tymoshenko and the latter were calling for her to be given a heavy prison sentence. Most protesters were paid to keep their flags flying in support of one or the other. The atmosphere was pretty surreal; people went from one camp to another because defectors were given bonuses. Not everyone was taking part for the money; there were some sincere protesters, but mostly, it was all a put-on job.

So we decided to protest against this whole murky business that divided Ukraine and drew the attention of the populace away from the problems of society. We appealed to reason, so that people would stop playing any part in these dirty political games. We wanted our message to be heard: beware, citizens, nobody ever thinks about you!

On 11 October 2011, when the verdict went against Yulia Tymoshenko, thousands of her supporters flooded into Khreshchatyk Avenue. We climbed on to the roof of the Tsum[3] department store, and there we hung our banner, so it would cover the first letter of the sign.[4] Oksana had drawn a big button on it, like those used to connect an electrical appliance. It was a play on words, a pun: 'Plug into your reason!', as *um*, that is, the letters that we hadn't concealed, means 'reason'. And we yelled: 'Yu (Yulia) and Ya (Yanukovych), the same filth!' This was written on one of our banners too.

In the West, people have a very idealistic image of Tymoshenko, but the reality is quite different. She's a predator from the caste of oligarchs who bet on Yushchenko during the Orange Revolution, but they are actually different. Yushchenko has class, although he's a bad manager who failed to understand the priorities of our country. Before initiating projects of a historical and cultural character, such as obtaining international recognition of the Ukrainian famine,[5] it was necessary to give people bread and work. Yushchenko would have been more in place in Poland or another European country.

As for Tymoshenko, what would have happened if she'd won the last presidential election? True, there has been a significant reduction in liberties since Yanukovych came to power, and we continue to fight tirelessly against this, but we do not believe, in all honesty, that Tymoshenko would have preserved the freedoms and principles of the Orange Revolution if she'd taken power. She's an autocrat; she'd never have given anyone a chance to deviate an inch from her plans. Without her time in prison, she'd have lost all her prestige and all her authority. Her imprisonment may perhaps change her for the better. However, we cannot exclude the possibility that she'll throw Yanukovych in jail, if she one day becomes president. He deserves it as much as she does: they're both criminals locked in combat with each other. Of our number, Sasha is the one with the most radical views of Tymoshenko:

For me, the Orange Revolution remains a source of inspiration and a great memory. However, it's difficult for me to associate Tymoshenko positively with this revolution. How was Tymoshenko better than Yanukovych? She was pretty, she dressed elegantly, and she wore high heels. So? Has she ever raised the issue of the status of women? Has she contributed to gender equality? The answer is no!

Today, she complains of the violence in prison. We ourselves have gone through this terrible experience and we know the statistics – they're dreadful. Even just in the police stations, more than one hundred people per year die of torture during 'strenuous' interrogations. And I'm not even talking about violence in the prisons! So why didn't she look into this problem when she was prime minister? Nowadays she only ever talks about herself, of the few blows she's suffered, instead of denouncing the condition of all prisoners. She presents herself as a heroine who's done time in jail when she could have saved the country. Why didn't she tried to save it earlier?

FIRST EUROPEAN TOUR

In 2010, we met a Swiss director who became a friend: he's followed us everywhere since then. His name is Alain Margot. He began by making a programme about us for Swiss television and then he decided to make a documentary, *Femen – Our God is a Woman* – which should come out in cinemas in 2013.

It was during our discussions with him that the idea of going on tour in various European countries was born. Before then, while staying in Kiev, we'd already organized actions around international topics, as with our support for Sakineh Mohammadi Ashtiani. But it's one thing to imagine, while in Ukraine, what's going on in the West, and quite another to see things with our own eyes and talk to people. As we are positioning ourselves as defenders of European values, democracy and feminism, we were very eager to tour in Europe. We persuaded Alain Margot that this tour would give a new angle to the film, and it was his producer who financed the trip.

We discussed our itinerary at length with Alain, and the

themes that we could address in different countries. There
were four of us undertaking this journey: Sasha, Inna, Jenia
Kraizman and Anna. We first arrived in a small Swiss town,
La Chaux-de-Fonds, where Alain lives. On 29 October
2011, we gave a lecture about our struggle and participated
in debates at the town's Club 44 where cultural events take
place. It's a well-known discussion group in Switzerland; in
the past, it's hosted Jean-Paul Sartre, Simone de Beauvoir,
François Mitterrand and other celebrities. In front of a huge
audience – the 300-seat room was full – including politicians and journalists, we talked about our movement, in the
form of a master class, and Alain presented sequences of his
future film to illustrate our actions. This first discussion with
Europeans was really exciting, and lasted until midnight. We
seem to have won over some hearts and minds, and gained
the trust of the audience. There were two Ukrainian women
there who said that we were the only girls trying to change
the image of Ukrainian women in the eyes of Europeans.

After Switzerland, we went to Paris with the idea of tackling Dominique Strauss-Kahn. After Berlusconi, DSK was
another example of the unwholesome lifestyle so prevalent among the pundits of politics and finance. We learned
from French feminists where this character lived and on 31
October 2011, we went knocking on his door, at 13 place
des Vosges. We were wearing short black and white skirts,
like the women cleaners in the Sofitel where DSK committed his crime. We were armed with buckets, cloths, brushes
and brooms, in short, all the household utensils for cleaning
up dirt. Our inscriptions read: 'Drunk on power', 'Fuck me!',
and 'No whitewash for shame'.

When we started to scrub away at the door of DSK's
apartment block, making a huge rumpus, the domestics
there called the police but, unlike the Ukrainian police, the
French police were rather courteous. They wished us good

luck and quickly left. However, one thing did surprise us. In Ukraine, journalists filming or photographing in the street don't acknowledge the expression 'It's forbidden'. Whatever they're told by the police, they continue their work. This is a legacy of the Orange Revolution which has survived in spite of censorship. However, in Paris, when the police asked them to stop filming, everyone quickly obeyed.

And there's one more detail. It was during this brief trip to France that our motto was born: 'We came, we stripped, we conquered!' Of course, this is inspired by the quote *veni vidi vici*.

Two days later, we went to Rome. On 6 November 2011, we participated in a protest against Prime Minister Berlusconi organized by the Democratic Party on San Giovanni Square. Inna, Jenia and Sasha had first daubed their faces and bodies with green, white and red paint, the colours of the Italian flag. We wore slogans in Italian and in English: 'Silvio, che cazzo fai?'[6] and 'Fuck Berlusconi!' So we were joining forces with the Italian left as they demanded the immediate resignation of this misogynist who had no qualms about using the sexual services of an underage girl. Berlusconi is a disgrace to Italy. The protesters were very enthusiastic and they shouted 'Brava, bella!' What a difference from the way we'd been greeted in Kiev!

However, the great action we called 'The Hammer of the Witches'[7] was yet to come. The next day, we went to St Peter's Square in the Vatican to put on our performance when the Pope said the Angelus from the balcony. We wanted to protest against the medieval, misogynistic policy of the Holy See, worthy of the Middle Ages, which forbids its followers to resort to contraception and abortion, and lobbies in Catholic countries to deprive women of their basic rights. This was one of the actions that left the deepest mark on Sasha:

I was finally forced to act alone, as other girls had been turned back at the entrance to the square. Apparently, the security service of the Vatican had heard of our plans. As usual, we had called a press conference and someone must have betrayed us. I was wearing a red jacket and walked beside Alain Margot. When I saw security barring the girls' way, I quickly donned Alain's jacket and we embraced like a couple of lovers. It was a simple but effective ploy. The guards were looking for a big blonde in the crowd, but they hadn't thought about couples. We entered the square safely, with a huge camera. There were many people in civilian dress speaking into walkie-talkies and on their mobile phones, while scanning the crowd. We played two lovers: I kept laughing and Alain filmed me. I didn't know what was happening to the other girls because we'd lost contact. We hadn't thought of buying prepaid Italian SIM cards, and our Ukrainian mobiles were unusable abroad. For us, this was a huge lesson, and I have to confess frankly that, on this occasion, we let ourselves down.

Meanwhile, the Pope was already coming to the end of his prayer on the balcony, and I realized that if I did nothing there and then, the journalists we'd asked to attend would leave. But there were police standing near the group of journalists and I couldn't signal to them. The placard was in Alain's bag. He took it out while I grimaced desperately at the press. Finally, one of the journalists saw me and they all ran over to us. It was a very strange feeling to me, being alone in the middle of such a huge square. I hastily stripped and yelled 'I'm free!' with such force that I felt I'd burst. The slogan on the placard was simple: 'Freedom for women!' I was wearing a transparent coat, sewn up like a nun's habit. The carabinieri jumped on me and covered me to prevent my arrest being filmed. I struggled, trying to free myself, but it was impossible: there were a dozen of them.

I was kept at the police station for two hours at most. I was told that my behaviour was considered to be hooliganism as I'd been topless in a sacred place, and that my case would go to court in a year or two's time. Much good may it do them! What matters is that it was our first antireligious protest. We'd already realized what a destructive influence religion has on the status of women at the time we studied Marxism. Personally, I always believed that sooner or later we would tackle religion. To do this, our first movement had to gain momentum and reputation so as not to scare and turn off those who support us. This had now been achieved, and the path we were following would soon show itself to be a fruitful one.

FEMEN SUPPORTS THE RUSSIAN OPPOSITION

For us, December 2011 was a very busy month. We'd decided to organize an action in Moscow where mass protests against Putin and the rigged elections to the Duma on 4 December were taking place.[8] After the results were announced, the first major event had been scheduled for 10 December, on Bolotnaya Square in the city centre. Our action was scheduled for the eve of this rally, before the great Cathedral of Christ the Saviour where the Russian establishment goes to pray. As the leader of this action, Inna was very concerned because there was every chance that the activists involved would be jailed for two weeks – this is the maximum sentence for 'non-aggravated hooliganism'. However, we'd already planned an action in Belarus for 19 December.

Let's hear Inna describe what happened:

In fact, we shared out our roles in a way that's still in operation today. So Anna deals with legal issues, paperwork and press releases; Oksana creates the whole visual side of our actions; Sasha and I do the head-hunting – we seek out future activists, train them and show them what to do on actions. You might even say that Sasha and I compete to see who can find the largest number of volunteers, although the task is daunting. It's very difficult to explain to young Ukrainian women what we do and why, so the number of recruits is an indicator of our professionalism.

So I needed to find two volunteers for our action in Moscow. However, everyone was afraid to go, as the Russian police, people say, are no joke. I found a wonderful girl and prepared her for action. This was my victory – in one week, I'd trained a true warrior! There was also another activist, Mariana, who'd been with us for a year, and she joined us. Anna came along with us but she wasn't taking part in the action as she needed to ensure the presence of the media and, in case of arrest, find us a lawyer and look after us.

On 9 December, it was very cold. The three of us made our way to the Cathedral of Christ the Saviour. Close to the entrance, we took off our winter coats and stood there with our torsos naked, and with Orthodox crosses painted in black on our breasts. We were also wearing medium-length jute canvas shorts, and on our buttocks Oksana had drawn two-headed eagles[9] and a bear, the logo of United Russia. We unfolded our placard that read: 'God, remove the Tsar!', and began yelling the same slogan – though the Tsar was, of course, Putin. Then we began to wave around whips and crosses made out of branches, as if we were carrying out an exorcism. We even crawled around on the ground for ten minutes, until the custodians of the cathedral came out and started hitting us while trying to cover us with big black refuse bags. Some women believers who were entering or leaving the cathedral also dealt us a few blows. We fought them off as best we could. After half an hour, the police still hadn't shown up. We then got dressed and left. Three police cars arrived five minutes after we left!

In retrospect, you might think that our action triggered Pussy Riot's. Two months later, they put on their performance in the same cathedral, with a similar slogan: 'Holy Virgin, chase Putin out!'[10]

We believe that our action was well designed, with a short, sharp slogan. We wanted to show solidarity with the Russian opposition in its fight against the rigged elections, and its endeavour to create a Russia without crooks or thieves,[11] but also without political prisoners. For us, this fight is very close to ours. However, the reaction of the Russians shocked us. When dispatches describing our work were published on the Internet, many bloggers and Internet users made scathing remarks. Their comments were of the kind: 'These poor Ukrainian girls, why are they interfering? We don't need their support, we'll solve our problems ourselves.' They're too proud of being Russian, too imbued with their imperialism, and they hate us because the Ukrainians are no longer part of their empire. Post-Soviet Russia suffers from paranoia: it sees itself as surrounded by enemies and is erecting a new Iron Curtain around itself, whereas today's world is so open and permeable.

8

IN BELARUS

A Dramatic Experience

In summer 2011, members of the Belarusian opposition who had fled the Lukashenko regime[1] arrived in Kiev. These people were not radical revolutionaries. What needs to be understood is that, in Minsk, you need just to step out into the street and clap your hands, and you'll get arrested. These members of the opposition came to the Cupid to get to know us and they brought us some Belarusian vodka – it was very good, actually. We met up several times. They told us horror stories about the Belarusian prisons – for example, the way the *spetsnaz*[2] train by using detainees as punch-balls. They also told us about Lukashenko's 'death squads',[3] as well as a very violent dispersal of his opponents, which occurred 19 December 2010, after the announcement of the re-election of Lukashenko to a fourth term. Hundreds of people had been arrested, including all the other candidates!

Inna and Oksana decided to carry out an action against the tyrant in Minsk itself. Here, Inna relates this experience, which almost went badly wrong:

I was very angry about the tyrant, I wanted to yell and cry. There are situations that literally make my activist's blood boil. I unhesitatingly decided to go to Belarus and carry out an action on 19 December 2011, to commemorate the anniversary of the repression and support Belarusian political prisoners. The big question was who would join me.

We scratched our heads long and hard over this. Oksana sometimes seems to have her head in the clouds; she can be difficult to understand, especially since she's not very talkative, but she's a radical activist, a girl who'll go to the bitter end for a real cause. She was scared, as I was, but we both knew that we were going through with it. Who'd be the third? We needed to find her quickly because time was running out. While desperately looking round, I suddenly remembered a young woman in Donetsk, Aleksandra Nemchinova, who'd participated in one action at my side. True, she weighs 120 kilos and doesn't really fit the Femen image. However, for this specific action, she had the perfect profile.

We didn't know how to tell her that our idea was for her to play Lukashenko during a topless protest in Minsk . . . I was so afraid of her reaction that my hand shook as I dialled her number. She was shocked by the proposal; she didn't know how to react. Like a dictator, I gave her twenty minutes to think it over. If she agreed, she'd need to take the train to Kiev that evening. The next day, we had to leave for Minsk with a detour via Bryansk, in Russia, to avoid the need for a Belarusian visa.

The next morning, Aleksandra came to the Cupid. I'd warned her that we'd be topless but I hadn't told her that we'd be shaving her head and dressing her up in a military uniform to make her look like Lukashenko . . . Anyway, once she was in Kiev, she really had no choice. We bought the uniform from a store for officers: a pair of trousers,

epaulettes, belt, and boots. The closer we got to the time
we were due to leave, the more scared we felt. Our journalist friends told us: 'You're crazy. You'll never come back,
they'll kill you there.' Two hours before we set off, we
returned to the Cupid where a photographer had set up his
stand. We decided to have our photos taken – as a souvenir,
I joked.

In the evening, we took a train to Bryansk. Many people
came to the station to say goodbye. Everyone was very
emotional. In the process, we started to think how we
should behave if they beat us with batons. We'd watched
a video where the Belarusian KGB were smashing the skull
of a young woman dissident. We agreed that we should
stop all resistance once they took out their clubs. During
this discussion, Oksana received a text message from Sasha:
'Don't worry! If you get your teeth smashed in, we'll all
raise money on Facebook to pay for a new set.' This black
humour fell flat. We were all so on edge!

Before the border control, we told ourselves that if
I was recognized and forced off the train, Oksana and
Aleksandra would carry out the action, just the two of them.
Everything went well but, as a precaution, we pretended we
weren't travelling together. After a complicated journey via
Bryansk, then a small Belarusian town, we finally arrived in
Minsk the next day at 5 a.m.

A group of policemen was standing at the station
entrance. Unlike the paunchy, oafish Ukrainian police,
these ones seemed to be well trained and threatening, with
big clubs. Aleksandra told me that she had a moment of
panic and almost did a runner. 'I'm admitting this so you
won't doubt me. I'm ready, I know why we're doing this.
It's my decision,' she told me. I was relieved. This girl had
the makings of a hero.

Kasia was expecting our call. She's the correspondent

for an opposition radio station based in Poland and she'd agreed to meet us at her home. She fixed a rendezvous point near a cinema and took us to her flat through narrow streets, as if she was a conspirator. Our action was planned for 11 a.m.

At 11 o'clock, we took a taxi and drove round the square where the KGB building was. We'd alerted a number of foreign journalists, but the square seemed empty. Then we saw three journalists with TV cameras and another two on the other side of the square. I shouted: 'It's kicking off!'

We hastily stripped and disguised Aleksandra as Lukashenko. All three of us were topless, with written slogans on our bodies. Our banners proclaimed: 'Long live Belarus!' and 'Freedom to political prisoners!' Aleksandra, tall and strong, had a shaven skull and a thick moustache and we'd glued fake eyebrows on her. Oksana had drawn, on her back, a portrait of Lukashenko, and on her abdomen, a red star. She was sensational!

While we continued yelling slogans, two women journalists walked past us and took some pictures without stopping. I asked myself: 'Why are they leaving?' The four or five other journalists continued to photograph and film us. Among them, there was an Australian director, Kitty Green, who was making a film about us. Suddenly, the main door to the KGB building opened and two guys with walkie-talkies emerged. The third, a hefty guy like those at the railway station, strode towards us, waving his baton around vigorously. We were standing 10 metres from the KGB entrance on a raised porch, and he shouted: 'Get down right now!' My knees were shaking, but we didn't move. Five men came to join him. They surrounded us and grabbed the journalists, including Kitty. Apparently, the KGB people had decided to arrest the journalists and destroy their photos and videos. In any case, we got dressed again and nobody followed us.

We found Kasia near the cinema. Filled with exultation, we embraced and even rolled around on the asphalt. We were free! We went back to Kasia's apartment and ordered a pizza while responding to hundreds of calls from journalists. However, I had a feeling that the story wasn't over yet. Kasia was also worried and asked us to leave as quickly as possible. She booked tickets for us in a bus to Gomel where we were supposed to catch a train to Kiev. We thought that the KGB would be waiting for us at the railway station in Minsk, not at the bus station.

We ordered a taxi. As soon as we got out, we noticed a man in a black coat, sitting on a bench in front of the entrance. At the bus station, we went to get our tickets at the counter. Again, there was a man in a black coat following us. In the waiting room, several people with headsets seemed to be watching us. We tried to reassure ourselves: the KGB just wanted confirmation that we were really leaving Belarus.

When our bus arrived, we joined the queue. It was at this point that ten men attacked us. In a few seconds, each of us was neutralized. I tried to scream but one of the guys covered my mouth with his hand. Four of them held me, searching my pockets and my bag. Just next to me there was a woman of about fifty quietly waiting for her bus. She could see the scene, she could see that I was being gagged, but her face expressed no emotion. I said to myself: this is what a totalitarian country is like.

They pushed me towards a silver minibus. Oksana, one of the kidnappers, and the driver were already inside. As for Aleksandra, she was shoved into a coach that followed us. The agents confiscated our mobiles and started to browse our SMS messages. They were not aggressive and didn't hit us. They asked us questions such as: 'Who are you? Who gave you the order to come here? Who thought up this action? Where did you spend the night?'

Finally, the minibus stopped in a yard. Two or three cars arrived, including the one carrying Aleksandra. The guys carried on questioning us and getting 'preachy'. They said: 'You bitches, you don't know what you're meddling with. You're playing into the hands of Europe, where they do whatever they can to denigrate the Slavic people. Yes, our people have a hard life but we're opposed to capitalism, in Europe and in the United States, and we will win! We, the Slavs, will never give in to an America that wants to dominate the world!'

This was exactly their master's voice – Lukashenko's. During the interrogation, they tried to set us against each other. They said to Oksana and Aleksandra that I'd received huge sums of money to take them to Minsk and perform this action. To me, they said they knew all about me, and kept asking me who'd paid me, and how much. I was exasperated, and I decided to make a joke of it. When they asked me for the umpteenth time who'd paid me, I said, 'Mahatma Gandhi'. One of those guys took this badly: 'Inna, you're starting to really bug us with your jokes. You think I don't know who this woman, Mahatka Gandhi, is?' The three of us couldn't help but burst out laughing.

Then we set off again. Our captors took us to near the big library in Minsk that is all lit up at night-time, as if to show us how happy life is in this country. We remained for nearly five hours there, trapped in the minibus. The men went out to have a smoke, but we couldn't move and I dozed off. When I woke up, I asked what they would do to us, and they said: 'We don't know, we're waiting for orders.' At dawn, about 6 a.m., twelve hours after our arrest at the bus station, our minibus and the other cars drove off.

'Where are we going?'

'You'll see. We've been given our orders.'

Suddenly, the minibus stopped in front of a pinewood. One of our captors pushed Oksana's cap down on her head, to cover her eyes. Then he ordered us to get out, one after another.

Aleksandra was subjected to the same treatment but I didn't have a cap. He then made me get out and forced me to walk hunched and head bowed. He took me to another bus and pushed me towards a guy who twisted my arms behind my back and handcuffed me. His way of saying 'hello' was to tell me, 'You bitches are going to be punished for coming here and trying to break our national unity!'

Our captors handed us over to another group. The new bus had no normal seats, but two long benches along the sides. Each of us was flanked by two guys checking all our movements. In total, there were fifteen or so men in the new group of kidnappers, all hooded. They were silent, except for one who spoke non-stop. He was a real professional. He said:

'We're going to kill you. We'll enjoy butchering you for what you've done.' And he went further: 'Breathe! I want to hear your breathing. Your last hour's come. Remember your childhood, all the good times you experienced before coming here. Remember your Mom's smile. Imagine her face now, when she sees you dead and disfigured.'

It was a long journey. I tried to reassure myself, I kept telling myself that it was a professional intimidation, a game. If they wanted to kill us, why were they hooded? I was hoping they'd take us to the border and release us. My body was hurting horribly because I was tied up. But every time I moved my shoulders, I was punched on my neck or my back.

Oksana and Aleksandra needed to go to the toilet and

asked for the bus to stop. My two captors dragged me out too, to the edge of the road:

'Go on!'

'What?'

'You gonna piss?'

'No.'

They took me back inside the bus and threw me on to the bench. The journey continued for hours on end. When the bus finally stopped, we were on the edge of a thick forest. They dragged us about 100 metres to a clearing, where they removed our handcuffs. They stood in a semi-circle round us, all hooded. Two men started filming us with two cameras. Three or four men were holding pillows. Another leaned casually on a shovel. And another, really close up to me, was playing with a long sharp knife. It was surreal!

The 'chatty' one told us in a threatening tone of voice to do everything we were ordered to do:

'If you don't, we'll kill you!"

They ordered us to strip and remain topless. Then they gave us placards with swastikas on and ordered us to hold them, like during an action. The 'chatty' one commented on camera:

'Look at these chicks who travel round the world performing their number. Look at their placards!'

The man with the knife came close up to me: 'Look straight into the camera and smile!'

Then he ordered us to get dressed, adding that he'd count up to three. If we were not dressed after three, he'd kill one of us. Several times, he made us get dressed and then undressed again.

'One, two, three!'

When we were once again topless, another man approached us and poured motor oil from a jerry can all over us. The 'chatty' one kept up his commentary to camera. Then one of our captors took out a lighter as if he wanted to turn us into living torches. A game, of course! Then this same guy ordered us to take off our trousers and knickers.

'Now turn round and bend over!'

I thought they were going to rape us from behind, but they just hit us with sticks. All this was filmed. Then the man with the knife came over and started cutting off my long hair, strand after strand. It was horribly painful. He threw my locks at my feet. Then he poured over my head some *zelionka*, a green dye that's used as a disinfectant in our part of the world. My face and what was left of my hair took on a dark green colour. Then he put a few drops on Aleksandra's shaven head. Finally, the guy with the knife ripped open the pillows and dumped feathers on us. What a macabre performance! Apparently, the Belarusian KGB had decided to respond to our action tit for tat, as it were. And to pass this video on to their 'boss', Lukashenko.

Finally, they ordered us to get dressed. We were oiled, painted green, covered with feathers. We were shoved into the bus. The 'chatty' one approached me with the camera:

'How do you feel?'

'OK.'

'Will you be coming back to Belarus?'

'We'll see when we get back to Kiev.'

I said this without thinking. I thought that he'd hit me but he just stopped filming, without saying a word. Oksana began to sob convulsively. It was a nervous reaction. A quarter of an hour later, the bus stopped in the middle of a big forest at the edge of a ravine. At the bottom, we could see a river. I thought they were going to throw us into the river, but they told us to walk through the forest for 15 to 20 kilometres, as far as the Ukrainian border. Then they left.

I asked Oksana: 'What are you crying for?'

'I realized it was over.'

'It's not over yet. They may be waiting for us in this forest. This is no time to crack.'

This forest was the wildest place I'd ever seen. Snow, swamps where we kept sinking in. Aleksandra found it very difficult to walk because she suffers from a knee problem. After two or three hours of walking, we realized we were going round in circles. Night would soon be falling. Fortunately, we managed to find the place where those guys had abandoned us, on a small road. It was already dark when we met a group of lumberjacks returning home after a day's work. They looked us warily up and down – we looked pretty weird, to put it mildly.

From a distance, we followed them to their small village, a totally isolated place. We knocked on a door and an old man opened up and introduced himself as 'Uncle Sasha'. He allowed us to use his mobile. First I called Mom and I said, in a cheerful voice:

'Hi, Mom, I lost my mobile, everything's OK.'

'You're alive!'

For the previous twenty-four hours, all the Ukrainian TV channels had been talking about our disappearance in Belarus. After this conversation with my mother, it was my turn to break down in tears, as Oksana had done shortly before. Still, I phoned Anna so she would quickly alert our ambassador in Belarus, because I was afraid that our captors might come back.

Meanwhile, Uncle Sasha had cooked us some pasta with grilled onions and given us his jeans and socks so we could change. He even washed my hair in a tub, but the green dye wouldn't come out. My face was just as green too. A lumberjack of about thirty, with huge hands, totally drunk, suddenly burst into the house, saying he wanted to 'fuck' us. This was all we needed! Uncle Sasha managed to throw him out. We were in a state of extreme exhaustion. We were trembling in spite of the quilts our host had wrapped around us. Anna called me back to tell us that the Ukrainian consul was already on the way, but he needed time to get to this place in the back of beyond.

A police patrol came quickly looking for us. Several foreign journalists and the Ukrainian consul were waiting for us at the police station. We wanted to lay a complaint against our captors, but the consul told us to leave straightaway. A man in a black coat prowled around watching us and observing what was happening. The signal was clear. At dawn, we returned to Kiev in the consular car – our only escape route since, as our ID had been confiscated, we'd never have been able to cross the border.

Anna and Sasha welcomed us warmly. The press conference took place at 2 p.m. in the Cupid. The room was crowded, and media interest helped us to overcome our emotional shock. The Belarusian KGB had failed to destroy all the photos of our action. Those two journalists who had taken some snapshots in passing, before the KGB turned up, had made them available. A good tactic! As for Kitty Green's film, computer technicians in Australia were able to restore her memory card that had been erased by the KGB: sixty hours of footage in total, including our action.

For the first days after our return to Kiev, I was afraid to go out. I felt I was being followed. Today, I believe that those twenty-four hours in the hands of my kidnappers were the most intense moments in my life. It's the kind of event that allows you to realize who you really are. You expect to be killed at any moment. It's said that people see their lives passing before their eyes before dying. That's what happened to me, and not for a single second did my commitment weaken, nor did I doubt what I was doing. So yes, it was the most horrible day in my life, but also the best.

Inna kept her promise to the 'chatty' one, since on 1 July 2012, in Kiev, we organized a new action against Lukashenko when he came to the Olimpiyskiy Stadium for the finals of Euro 2012. We were topless, hooded, and did a dance with batons round Aleksandra who again played the role of the Belarusian dictator.

9

FEMEN GETS RADICAL

ATTACK IN DAVOS

When we decided to carry out an action in Davos at the World Economic Forum, some of our friends tried to convince us that it wasn't for us. But what's the good of talking about the global crisis if women's voices are not taken into account? Women are the first victims of the crisis. It's they who are the poorest and least protected. It's as feminists, as 'naked women', that we intended to perform a radical action against the rich, against those who plunge entire populations into poverty. We wanted to denounce this global economic conspiracy of the most powerful men in the world who meet up to feast in a time of famine. If we limited ourselves to purely feminine issues, we'd quickly get dragged into futile discussions, such as the need to 'feminize' the names of various professions, such as 'writeress' or 'professoress'. This makes us mad!

Four of us travelled to Switzerland: Anna, Sasha, Oksana

and Inna. As usual, we planned an action for three of us, with Anna to guard our rear and establish links with the press. The anti-globalization protesters and anarchists had camped 40 kilometres from Davos and everyone said we wouldn't get through the safety barriers. Despite that, we were determined to find a way to slip into the 'wolves' lair'. We had three slogans: 'Poor because of you', 'Gangsters party in Davos' and 'The crisis: *made in Davos*'.

We'd learned the lesson from our half-botched action at the Vatican. When Inna had turned up near the Holy See in make-up, with her blonde hair, she'd immediately been recognized and locked up. Since then, we've been more cunning, and we disguise ourselves in hats, glasses and coats so as to go unnoticed. Inna even dyed her hair black to escape the vigilance of the guards during our actions at Euro 2012.

To go to Davos, we'd invented this scenario: we were a group of actors accompanied by a cameraman, Alain Margot. We bought train tickets as far as a small town where we spent the night of 27 to 28 January 2012. To reach Davos, we thought of renting a car, but as this would have been very expensive we continued by train. All the information we'd been given was false: there was no identity check on the train to Davos, and we got there unhindered. The place was blanketed in snow, and empty.

We went into a small cafe. On the train, we'd phoned journalists to warn them that an action would take place in three hours. As we didn't know exactly where to go, we sent Oksana and an interpreter to reconnoitre. They returned crestfallen:

'Girls, we're screwed. There are snipers around the building and also on the roof. They're all armed with automatic rifles. If we make one movement too many, they'll shoot.'

For five seconds, we remained in shock. Then we started to develop a plan. The idea was to get off the bus which passes near the building, very slowly remove our coats and jackets, unfold our placards so they could see that they were made of paper and we weren't terrorists, then move forward very slowly, peacefully, above all without screaming. We tried to keep our spirits up, but we were scared: if the snipers sensed the least threat, they could shoot.

An hour later, we met up with the journalists and took the bus which, as expected, stopped near the building. We ran to the entrance, forgetting the danger and the instructions we'd drawn up in the cafe, and we tried to climb the enclosure mesh. The snipers observed us, but didn't shoot. The police even waited a quarter of an hour before arresting us. The arrest itself was rough, we were handcuffed and shoved into a police van. Sasha was terrified and kept repeating, 'They're going to kick us out, they'll cancel our Schengen visas. We'll never be able to carry out another action in Europe.'

At the police station, we were very kindly received. The police told us they knew who we were as they'd seen us on TV, and they liked us. They even offered us tea as we were chilled to the bone. It was a few degrees below zero. They confiscated all our placards, adding that we could pick them up the next day, and they let us go. You should have seen how surprised Sasha was! The free world really is an extraordinary place!

NO TO RUSSIAN GAS IMPERIALISM!

Throughout the winter of 2012, Russia conducted a gas war against Ukraine. It was a terribly harsh winter and in Ukraine, 135 people died because of the exceptional cold. Many Ukrainian households couldn't pay the exorbitant price for Russian gas. The Ukrainian government then offered to renegotiate this price with Moscow to bring it down, but Russia was ready to accept only if it could seize the whole

Ukrainian gas network. For Putin, the gas valve became a weapon of blackmail used to bind Ukraine more tightly to Russia. We decided to act against Gazprom, demanding that Russia stop manipulating our country. This was the tenor of our news release: 'We demand that Putin stop forcing Ukraine into a Euro-Asian cohabitation!'

On 13 February 2012, there were five or six of us in Moscow. We hadn't slept all night so we could stay together and not miss the plane. The flight was at 6 a.m., and we had to be at the airport at 4 a.m. In Moscow, it was extraordinarily cold: 32 degrees below zero, and we were completely shattered. We went straight to the Gazprom offices. They have a huge tower block in the city centre, and the entrance is jealously guarded by a pack of watchdogs. We carried out a diversionary tactic, topless, with signs that said 'Stop the gas blackmail!' and 'Close down Gazprom!' While the guards tried to catch us and neutralize us, Oksana, who is amazingly agile and supple, managed to climb on to the checkpoint and hang the Ukrainian flag on its roof. The rest of us decamped quickly as the police hadn't shown up yet, but Oksana couldn't follow us. She had to climb down, and this took time. She took refuge in a building on the other side of the square, but local journalists informed the police. We couldn't understand this reaction. In Kiev, journalists sometimes give the game away so as to film a juicy story, such as 'How the cops arrest a girl from Femen'. But here, the guys didn't even take any photos; it was pure sadism.

Oksana was questioned extensively by agents of the FSB. Later, we learned that all the guards were sacked because we'd managed to cross the barrier. We even felt sorry for the poor buggers. Oksana was kept for several hours at the police station, after which she was entitled to a special meeting of the administrative court at 3 a.m. It imposed a fine of

3,500 roubles and allowed her to leave. It was the first time she'd been arrested.

Sasha has very fond memories of this episode:

> It was the first time we'd carried out an action in such freezing weather, topless, as usual. On our way there, we wondered how we'd manage not to drop dead because of the cold. But when we took off our clothes, and we each had a job to do, we suddenly no longer felt either cold or afraid. In these moments, we're filled with such exaltation, such joy, that our physical abilities seem multiplied tenfold. Take me: I'm not very sporty, but during the action, I can run like a hare and climb where I'd never have normally managed. That's Femen: the intoxicating feeling of total freedom and the joy of being together, with our comrades in arms, ready for anything. I'd say that's what happiness is. And it's this happiness that makes Femen radiant and beautiful.

10

'I'M STEALING PUTIN'S VOTE!'

Although reactions to our 'God, chase away the Tsar!' demo of December 2011 had rather burnt our fingers, we again supported the Russian opposition in its protest against electoral fraud in the general election and against Putin's return to power. Four of us went to Moscow: Oksana, two new activists – another Anna and Ira – and Anna was there, as usual, to look after the logistics. Naturally, we weren't sure Oksana would manage to get through passport control unimpeded. She'd been arrested barely three weeks earlier, after the action against Gazprom, but apparently the Russian police weren't expecting her to return so soon, and her name didn't appear on the blacklist of the border guards at the airport.

The idea was simple. The day of the first round of the presidential election on 4 March 2012, we arrived at the polling station in the building of the Academy of Sciences, on Lenin Avenue, where Putin had voted twenty minutes before, for himself of course. We succeeded in getting accreditation as journalists, with fake press cards. Without this trick, we wouldn't have managed to get in, since access to a polling station in Russia is only open to people in the constituency or to journalists and accredited observers. We quickly stripped and tried to remove the urn where Putin had put his ballot paper, screaming: 'I'm stealing Putin's vote!' and 'Putin is a thief!' We wanted to draw attention to the state of Russian democracy, where the presidential campaign had been moronic, the vote rigged and where, in any case, people had no freedom of choice since the real opponents hadn't been able to participate in the elections. The people facing Putin were just puppets. Our bodies were covered with inscriptions saying 'Putin is a thief!' and 'Rats from the Kremlin'.[1]

The station was under close guard and if we'd been there earlier, when Putin was there, we'd have certainly been killed. But now the guards just hurled themselves at us, trying to cover our nakedness. At the station, the FSB agents made us undergo a lengthy interrogation. We felt like we were going through our Belarusian adventure all over again. It was clear that, to their minds, the cold war between Russia and the West was still going strong. They told us:

'Why do you want to undermine the unity of the Slav world? Europe and the United States want to conquer us, and you're just traitors. Who's put you on to this? How much does the CIA pay you for these nasty tricks?'

The whole conversation was of the same kind. By decision of the court, Oksana was sentenced to fourteen days in prison, Anna ten and Ira five. They were transferred to Special Prison No. 1, Fruktovaya Street, and handcuffed. Each girl was entitled to three guards and their own car, escorted by two other vehicles. So nine police cars were mobilized to transport them to prison, at a speed of 150 kilometres per hour, with flashing lights, as if they were very dangerous terrorists.

In the prison, they were forced to undress completely and undergo a body search during which women thoroughly inspected their mouths and anuses. Their possessions were also probed, millimetre by millimetre. During this humiliating procedure, men kept coming and going constantly. As they'd been brought in by the FSB, the guards themselves were nervous and took it out on them. It was a form of psychological pressure.

Oksana relates what it was like in jail:

They put me in the same cell as Ira, a new girl on her first action. As for Anna, she was placed in another cell where there was a woman sick with hepatitis C. In my cell, it wasn't much better. I shared it with a girl addict and an alcoholic. The mattresses and blankets were rotten and stank horribly. No daylight came in, and a light bulb was kept on day and night. We were monitored continuously through the peephole.

We were guarded by three teams that took turns every eight hours. The guards in the first two teams were nasty, but those in the third were more humane. Sometimes they talked to us and passed on the latest news. Psychologically, this was important for us, because what a prisoner suffers the most is the total lack of information, being cut off from society.

The guards woke us up at six in the morning by banging hard on the door. We had to make our beds, and had no right to sit or lie down on them during the day. There's nothing to do there, except read, but there was no chair or table and we had to remain standing. The minute we tried to sit down, the guards banged on the door and shouted: 'Stand up, you're not on holiday here!' We were also required to wash the floor every day. Shortly before our incarceration, there'd been an inspection from the health authorities who'd found that the prison was infested with cockroaches. A disinfection had been ordered, the ground and the lavatories in particular were littered with dead cockroaches. We were ordered to pick them up. I initially refused to do this work because it wasn't in the regulations, but the guards punished those who refused to obey by denying them access to the shower. I didn't have any choice.

The two women who shared my cell were constantly complaining that, because of us, they were also constantly being monitored. Although possession and use of laptops are strictly prohibited in prison, they'd been able to use theirs before our arrival. In our presence, it was no longer possible.

The young drug addict, Katya, suffered terribly from withdrawal symptoms; her body demanded a new dose. On the third day, she collapsed in front of me, while I was brushing my teeth. She was an epileptic. I tried to help by inserting my toothbrush in her mouth. With the other inmate, we turned her over to stop her choking. We banged on the door to get the guards to call a doctor. There wasn't a doctor, just a nurse on duty. As it was late in the day, she was about to go home, but she still came and gave Katya an injection of magnesium. We demanded that Katya be hospitalized, but she laughed at us. Ira and I spent the night watching over her because she was in really bad shape.

Yet I was happy to be in the cell where, six months ago, Edward Limonov[2] had been incarcerated. I asked the 'good' guards to tell us about him. 'A nice old bloke who stayed all day on his bed, writing,' they told me. Apparently he'd been treated better than us, because he had the right to use his bed in the daytime.

During our incarceration, Anna was great. She sent us food and books to keep our spirits up. Above all, she kept the journalists informed about everything that was happening to us.

In prison, FSB officers summoned me for daily interrogations. They kept saying that these fourteen days were only the beginning of our troubles because then we'd be transferred to a detention centre where conditions would be much worse. This is where we would feel how very guilty we were, because we'd stay there a month or two, until Ukraine paid Russia for our expulsion. In this prison, we'd be with 'black arses'[3] and as they'd been told we were a pack of sluts, we might not get out alive.

This prospect scared us but it was just an attempt at intimidation. Anna was waiting for me when I was released from prison, together with some journalists, but the police made me leave through a small side door. I was immediately placed in a car from the department of deportation and taken to the airport. They put me on a flight to Kiev, warning me that I'd no longer have the right to enter Russian territory. Ira and Anna suffered the same fate. As we'd been threatened with many things and as they hadn't put the necessary stamps in our passports, we thought this was an idle threat. In reality, it turned out to be correct: all three of us have been banned from entering Russia for five years.

It's unfortunate that the Russian opposition didn't appreciate our action at all, as in December 2011. Iranians and Belarusians sent us floods of letters after our actions in favour of their freedom, but not the Russians. In Russia, even simple people who do not benefit in the slightest from the regime in power feel a sort of nationalist and imperialist pride. This is largely due to the heavy historical heritage of the Russians. We Ukrainians are very different people. We never had a tsar. For us, power passed from hand to hand: Poles, Russians, and parts of Ukraine, Romanians and Hungarians, not to mention our many *hetmans.*[4]

The Ukrainians have learned to ignore the state, not to identify with it. We have no reverence for authorities and that is why it's difficult to impose authoritarian rule on us. You could say we have more of a European mentality. As for members of the Russian opposition, it's their isolation that's problematic. They don't support the Syrians, or the Belarusians, or anyone else. However, if you don't feel the pain of people from other nations, other sources, other cultures, you won't get anywhere in your own country. The Russians simmer in Putin's cauldron, they suffer, but they're still stuck with their imperial syndrome. What a mess!

11

NAKED RATHER THAN IN A NIQAB!

8 MARCH, IN ISTANBUL

As soon as you take a closer look at the scandals involving Islamists, you find that it's often a woman who's at the centre. Sometimes a little girl with Down's syndrome in Islamabad is accused of burning the Koran and this triggers pogroms in Christian neighbourhoods; sometimes huge demonstrations are organized all around the world due to a film, *The Innocence of Muslims*, demonstrations which create many victims; sometimes a girl in Pakistan gets six bullets in her head for writing a blog on the BBC website, and so on. These examples are legion, and we suspect that many of these stories are put up by Islamists themselves. The case of the Down's syndrome girl who miraculously escaped a death sentence with her parents is emblematic. In fact, it was a local imam who himself burned some pages of the Koran and stuffed them into the innocent girl's bag. Islamists exploit the feelings of believers to burn US Embassies and especially to kill women. In a part of the Muslim world, women are beaten, humiliated, deprived of their basic rights, sentenced to death by strangulation and stoning. When we read the news from Saudi Arabia or Iran, when we see pictures of women being tortured, we boil over with rage. How can we tolerate women being treated as slaves, raped, married off at the age of ten? If we think that human rights are universal, why do our Western societies remain indifferent to the plight of these women?

For a while, we'd felt an urge to perform an action in a Muslim country. It is one thing to protest against stoning in Ukraine, it's another to go out to where it's happening. We particularly wanted to do something for 8 March, International Women's Day, to express our pain and solidarity vis-à-vis mistreated Muslim women. We chose Turkey for our first 'on the spot' action because of a whole set of circumstances. On the one hand, we'd found a Turkish sponsor. He's the owner of a brand of women's lingerie that makes special bras for women who've undergone mastectomy, and he supports various social projects for women. He contacted us to say that he admired our struggle. He promised that he'd print, at his own expense, a significant number of our T-shirts – which he did – and organize our visit to Turkey, if we wanted. Let's admit frankly that this man also had a commercial interest: he was going to put his logo on the invitations to our press conference in Istanbul, where all the local and international press would be present. A damn good publicity stunt!

The choice of Turkey for our first action in the Muslim world seemed sensible. In Turkey, domestic violence against women happens daily, but it's also a country that has a long tradition of secularism and wants to join the European Union. We thought that our voice could be heard there. We also wanted to experiment in a Muslim country that is not too extreme. We would of course never have demonstrated topless in Iran!

On the eve of 8 March 2012, we arrived in Istanbul – the four of us, Inna, Sasha, Yana and Tatiana, and we held our press conference as scheduled. We stated that we would fight for the rights of Turkish women, and Sasha even expressed the hope that Turkish women would join our movement and perform actions to defend their freedoms. We also denounced cases where the Turks are involved in sex tourism in Ukraine. As for the action itself, we decided to offer the Turks 'an Asian cocktail'.

In front of the main mosque in Istanbul, Hagia Sophia, we stripped down to our knickers. Our bodies were painted as if they were covered with bruises and burns. Indeed, it's quite common in Turkey and other Muslim countries for women to get sprayed with acid as punishment for often imaginary 'crimes': this disfigures them for life. On our bodies and placards was written: 'H_2SO_4 – the formula of fear', 'Death to the barbarians!', 'Stop the acid attacks!', 'You've turned us into monsters', 'Why me?', 'Guilty because I'm a woman'.

The day before, we'd announced our action without specifying the time or place. However, the police were waiting for us at Hagia Sophia, so the action only lasted fifteen seconds, plus ten more seconds to arrest us. The Turks unleashed a good three-dozen well-trained and super-fast female officers on us. In the twinkling of an eye, they'd handcuffed us, thrown us into a van and taken us to the police station. There, the cops knew exactly who we were. After a few formalities, we were transferred to a detention centre for illegal immigrants awaiting deportation. In fact, it was a prison.

Our Turkish lawyer, Doan Subasi, wasn't allowed inside. We were left alone, shut away, in a state of total uncertainty. Finally, a man came in, his eyes gleaming with hatred. He waved a pair of handcuffs in front of our faces and started to humiliate us verbally. We didn't understand what he was saying, but his facial expressions, his gestures and the emotions on his face were frankly obscene. He behaved as if we were slaves or prostitutes that he'd hand-picked for delivery. After this 'introduction', prison guards dragged us upstairs. We resisted because we were afraid of being separated, and the men just gleefully started kicking us over and over.

Meanwhile, our lawyer – who's supported us for a long time – alerted the press, and two hours later, the same men came to apologize. We were all put together in a VIP cell with clean sheets. And they brought a meal: apples, potatoes and pasta. Apparently, the cops were scared of being denounced when we were let out.

The next day we were told we'd be deported immediately. They put us in a police car, still handcuffed. A group of journalists were waiting for us at the prison gates, with the intention of following us by car. The driver of our bus tried to shake them off; he was travelling at such a speed that we fell off our seats and rolled around on the vehicle floor. The bus driver also resorted to a diversionary tactic. At one point, the bus stopped near an airport terminal. The driver triggered the automatic door, as if the cops were going to drop us off. The journalists jumped out of their car but our bus immediately restarted. Finally, despite this subterfuge, the reporters caught up with us, and we had a few minutes to tell them about everything that had happened since our arrest. We were then put on a plane to Kiev, after they'd stamped our passports with a ban on us entering Turkish territory for twelve months.

But we hadn't been mistaken in considering Turkey as a relatively civilized country. A month later, the Istanbul public prosecutor refused to bring charges, even though the police had demanded this. He ruled that our protest wasn't a criminal act because 'the sexuality of the activists was displayed as a protest and indicated the real objective of this protest, namely violence against women.' Therefore, our nakedness could not be regarded as something indecent or illegal: this was the prosecutor's conclusion.

We were quite happy with this decision, and we even thought the ban on entry into Turkish territory might be cancelled, but this wasn't the case. Turkey still has a long way to go if it wants to join Europe.

'MUSLIM WOMEN, GET UNDRESSED!'

We carried out our action against DSK without involving French feminists, but this episode contributed to our popularity and our current French activist colleagues say they've been inspired by it. A few months later, we received an email from Safia Lebdi,[1] suggesting a joint action with her group of activists against the wearing of the burqa in France.

When we receive a proposal to go abroad for a protest, we don't refuse. If we are invited to attend a conference abroad, we always arrange to combine our participation with action. In this case, we were initially hesitant because Sarkozy's government had passed a law banning the wearing of the burqa in public places, and we didn't want to endorse anything Sarkozy did, even if we agreed with this law. Safia persisted, forcefully explaining her position in long conversations on Skype. As she's a woman of the left, we eventually came to an agreement. Together, we decided that the action would be in the name of Femen and we would write the press release.

So the four of us went to Paris: Inna, Sasha, Tatiana and Oksana. On 31 March 2012, our protest action took place on the square in front of the Trocadéro, with fifteen or so other women brought along by Safia. We arrived in niqabs which we then suddenly tore away to reveal ourselves topless, just in our knickers in fact, with slogans on our bodies and placards: 'Rather naked than in a niqab!', 'Muslim women, get undressed!', 'France, strip off your clothes!', 'The truth = naked!', 'I am free!', 'Islamist = sadist', 'I'm a woman and not an object!' This action wasn't very sophisticated, but the participation of women of Arab origin produced a strong effect. We were really enthusiastic about our new friends. They were not young woman students, but married women or divorcees, with children, who wanted to follow us. Wow!

In this tourist area, the action went forward quietly. The police didn't intervene and no Islamists showed up. We were happy that in a country with strong feminist traditions such as France, feminists were willing to adopt the Ukrainian form of pop feminism. Isn't it wonderful? It was then that the idea of anchoring Femen in France was born. In Safia's group, all the activists were very enthusiastic.

Usually when we visit a country and a group of local girls wants to join us, we agree on the choice of the person who will lead the movement in the country after our departure. Indeed, there are Femen groups in Brazil, Tunisia, the United States, Switzerland, Germany, and so on. In all these countries, girls go out topless, with crowns of flowers on their heads, to protest, but these actions are coordinated from Kiev. In France, Safia put herself forward as the local leader of Femen. We were delighted.

We saw Safia again at the opening of Euro 2012 in Warsaw on 8 June 2012. She joined us to protest outside the stadium where the festivities were taking place. One hour before this slutty ceremony began, our Franco-Ukrainian gang, topless and with the slogan 'Fuck Euro' on our bodies, barred access to the stadium to a crowd of fans, strafing them with foam extinguishers. Following this rather spectacular action, we thought about an action for the London Olympics, to protest against the decision of the Olympic Committee to allow Muslim women to participate in sports competitions in traditional dress. In our view, such support for Islamists is an insult to the Olympic spirit and to women's causes. Countries that stone women or inflict corporal punishment on them are not worthy to participate in the Olympics. In our press release, we mocked the Olympic Committee, by offering to introduce new sporting disciplines, such as playing football with the head of a decapitated woman being used instead of the ball, or a competition between teams of 'stone throwers'.

Since we didn't get a visa for Britain, it was decided that we'd send a French 'commando' of five people, led by Safia. In London, the girls wore sports gear, with the inscriptions 'No to *sharia*!' and 'Olympic shame!' It was almost impossible for them to get into the area where the marathon was being run, and so they performed their action on Tower Bridge. The police immediately arrested them and they were kept at the police station for nearly eleven hours.

To return to our trip to Paris: this was an opportunity to initiate a public debate on feminism today. What surprised us was the aggressiveness of some participants. Our great clash involved the wearing of the niqab. These women, some of whom are Muslims, spoke out against the burqa but considered that it could not banned because this would be undemocratic. They claimed that it was women's personal choice. For us, this idea is intolerable.

Islamists force little girls to cover themselves as soon as they start menstruating at the age of eleven or twelve. In practice, in Afghanistan for example, girls are often covered from the age of six years. They are accustomed to be covered and don't know what freedom of the body is. We are against this savagery in general; we think it should be left to girls to decide for themselves. If we ban the niqab up to the age of eighteen, the girl can choose when she comes of age, and knows her own mind. At age eighteen, having already experienced the sensation of her body free to breathe, she can decide whether or not to enclose herself in a shapeless bag which is nothing but a symbol of women's slavery imposed by men – fathers, big brothers, husbands and imams. It's just as futile to talk of the free choice of women to wear the niqab as it is to claim that they choose freely to become prostitutes.

While in Paris, we also decided to work together with Safia to create an international training camp for feminists. This was a lifelong dream that had no chance of being realized in Ukraine. After the discussion on the niqab, Hervé Breuil, director of a theatre that's also the site of an alternative cultural space, the Lavoir Moderne Parisien, located in the Goutte d'Or,* contacted Safia, offering to host us if we returned. Safia then informed him of our idea of creating a training centre. Hervé responded he could not give us all of the large space there, already used by many actors and painters, but we were welcome to share it with them in a spirit of community. At that time, the Lavoir was already facing the prospect of closure, and Hervé was doing everything in his power to organize the maximum number of events to attract the public and the media. He thought that our presence could provide him with an additional argument against ejection. For us, it was an incredible gift of destiny: free premises in central Paris. What more could we ask for?

EURO 2012: THE FINAL STRETCH

With the approach of Euro 2012, something extraordinary happened in Kiev. Every day, new sex clubs opened on the

---

* Area in northern Paris (the 18th arrondissement, near Montmartre) with a large population of African origins. (*Trans. note.*)

sites of cafes or shops that disappeared as if by magic, with enticing advertisements aimed at the chauvinist pigs from abroad who would soon invade the capital. Our worst fears were being realized. We had to continue to fight against this huge brothel that would open in Kiev, and elsewhere too, because the games would be taking place in many Ukrainian cities.

Before the start of the championship, a tour of the trophy was organized, like the one done for the Olympic flame. The cup was to be presented to the public in several major cities. Fans had the opportunity to be photographed for free with it. You had to queue, and when it was your turn, an automatic camera took a souvenir snapshot. Then everyone could find his picture on the website of the championship.

We decided to tackle this symbol of Euro 2012, which we called 'Euro-cocotte'.* For the first time, we trained in order to achieve our objective. It was a question of knocking over the 'cocotte'. We made a copy of the base on which the 'cocotte' was enthroned. For the 'cocotte' itself, we used a bucket. The goal was to run very fast while removing our T-shirts, then knock the 'cocotte' over. Two or three of our girls played the role of guards trying to prevent the runners from committing their 'crime'. All the activists who had planned to participate in these actions – we'd planned three – trained for two or three days.

The first action took place in Kiev on 12 May 2012, and our activist Yulia Kovpatchik managed to deceive the guards and drop the 'cocotte' on the Maidan. Yulia was arrested, but the ceremony was interrupted and the 'cocotte' was dam-

---

* *Cocotte* is the French word for a casserole dish, a pressure cooker, a 'sweety' (i.e., a term of endearment for a woman) and a 'tart' (i.e., prostitute). (*Trans. note.*)

aged. The second action was held in Dnipropetrovsk on 21
May. It was Inna's turn to knock over the 'cocotte':

For this action, I got a female journalist from *Marie Claire*
to accompany me – she'd wanted to take part but couldn't
get to Dnipropetrovsk until the day before.

They were waiting for us at every event related to Euro
2012. The guards, who had been given pictures of the main
activists of Femen, had even prepared sheets to cover us.
To trick them, I dyed my hair black, and was wearing my
Sunday best. As I moved forward in the queue with the
journalist and the photographer from *Marie Claire*, they
thought we were a family and we weren't stopped. At the
decisive moment, I removed my T-shirt and knocked over
the 'cocotte', with the base on to which it was screwed. The
French journalist also took off her T-shirt, but she had an
attack of the giggles, which made me furious. In the photos,
it looks like mere larking around.

Allowing someone to participate in our action who wasn't
properly prepared was a mistake. With time, everything had
become more physical. We'd started off by just standing
around with a placard and then moved on to actions where
we need to travel some distance and successfully climb,
jump, fix a banner and so on before being arrested. There's
nothing extraordinary in the tasks we assign ourselves, but
we must learn to be focused, fast, light and agile. Moreover,
as our actions have become more hard-core, psychological
preparation is now necessary. Our activists must be able to
shout their slogans with unfeigned hatred, instead of finding it funny and displaying blissful smiles.

Three days later, we managed to knock over the 'cocotte'
for the third time, in Lviv. One of our best activists, Yana
Zhdanova, knocked over the 'cocotte' on the main square,

which cost her five days in jail. It was Sasha who went to Lviv to greet her on her release from prison, with the placard 'Yana is our heroine'.

Yana's trials had not yet ended. On 15 June 2012, Yana, Sasha and another activist, Anna Bolshakova, arrived in Donetsk, to perform an action at the Ukraine–France match. Upon arrival, they were tailed by people who looked more like special service agents than plainclothes police. Trying to shake them off, the girls split up and each went a different way by public transport. Around 4 p.m., contact with them was lost and their phones were switched off. We were very worried because the Donbass region is the stronghold of a powerful Mafia clan which was one of the major sponsors of Euro 2012. The Mafia is a law unto itself.

The girls managed to get back in touch at around 1 a.m. In fact, they had been kidnapped by the SBU, and taken to the police station. The men who had taken Anna Bolshakova had struck her repeatedly in the face. All three had been subjected to nearly nine hours of interrogation. When Sasha asked, sarcastically, 'Are you afraid that we might attack Yanukovych?', an agent replied, 'We don't give a damn about Yanukovych, it's our boss that counts.' His boss was obviously the Mafia leader. Overnight, the girls were driven to the police station and put in a train bound for Kiev.

Of course, we spread the news of this scandalous kidnapping widely. The next day, the head of the press service of the Ministry of the Interior stated that no abduction had taken place. He said the girls had come to the police station by themselves and had remained voluntarily for two hours. Of course they hadn't been beaten. It was so grotesque: instead of carrying out a protest action, our girls were supposed to have gone to get some rest in the delightful company of the cops! We needed to react.

We called the head of the press, Mr Polishchuk, and introduced ourselves as journalists from a foreign TV channel who wanted to interview him about the work of the Ministry of the Interior during Euro 2012. We suggested he come out on to the porch of the Ministry at 4 p.m. He did come out, in a nicely ironed uniform, looking very smart. Five television cameras and photographers were waiting for him. He didn't smell a rat. Inna had decided to give him a little lesson:

When we plan our actions, we often count on human stupidity, and in particular in Ukraine, when it comes to our officials. And it works! Reporters surrounded the guy, who was only too happy to be getting media attention, while one of our activists acted as an interpreter. While he blahblahed away, I approached him and threw a custard pie in his face, shouting insults. We chose a very soft cake so we wouldn't hurt him. It was his punishment for his shameless lie. I left quietly; nobody tried to catch up with me.

The next day, Polishchuk declared he would bring a criminal complaint against me. In fact, we always act in the open and announce who it was that participated in this or that action. I was summonsed several times but the justice system didn't really know what to do. It was the only time I hadn't been topless; I'd just offended the guy by my gesture, but this wasn't a matter for the criminal law. In the end, I wasn't given a sentence. However, our protests before and during the championship earned us several arrests and short stays in prison. In my case, I spent two days in jail, not to mention the various beatings I suffered. The cops even briefly arrested our friend, the Australian director Kitty Green, as well as our new ally in Brazil, Sara Winter, who'd come to join us in Kiev.

On 29 June 2012, Oksana tried a bold action. During the semi-final between Germany and Italy, she climbed on to the 10-metre high screen for the retransmission of the game at the stadium. Wearing blue overalls, she was supposed to hang a huge vertical banner saying 'Fuck Euro 2012' from the screen and then slip down a rope to the ground. Too bad this action could not be carried out. Oksana did climb along the screen, but to get to the middle, she had to walk on a 15-centimetre wide plank, with a sheer drop. She hesitated, and these few seconds allowed the guards to catch up with her. Another example of the need to study every detail of our actions.

Did we achieve our goals by demonstrating, in Ukraine and abroad, against Euro 2012? When it was officially announced that Ukraine would host Euro 2012, the heavyweights of Ukrainian politics such as Serhiy Tihipko and Vitali Klitschko suggested legalizing prostitution, allegedly so as to respond to the expected influx of prostitutes, as this always happens during major sporting events across the world. Our politicians were ready to 'brothelize' the country in the interests of the sex industry. Financially, this might have been beneficial to the state, as legalized brothels would have paid taxes. But is that a reason for selling into slavery tens of thousands of young Ukrainian girls? We were the only people to rebel against this idea; the international press echoed our protests, and ultimately prostitution was not legalized. We do not deserve all the credit, but we did help to change attitudes on this issue.

FEMEN SOUND THE ALARM

In March 2010, the Greek-Catholic Church and the Catholic Church of Ukraine proposed that voluntary termination of pregnancy be banned. A member of the Rada, Andriy Shkil, was quick to echo this wish by bringing forward a Bill on the prohibition of induced abortion. It's true that Ukraine is near the top, worldwide, when it comes to this procedure: unofficial statistics show a figure of 30 million abortions since the country gained independence in 1991. However, by what right can the state and the Church prevent a woman from enjoying the free use of her body? If the state wants there to be more births, why doesn't it improve conditions for women? How can they force a woman who can't make ends meet to give birth to kids that she won't be able to deal with? How can they avoid a situation where a woman who doesn't want to be a mother resorts to charlatans who might simply butcher her? This hypocrisy is deeply shocking. Basically, the state is ready to support the Church, as the Church, for its part, uses its 'moral authority' to support the regime. You just have to see how Yanukovych flirts with believers!

We decided to carry out a spectacular action against this Bill during Holy Week. On 10 April 2012, just like tourists, four of us climbed up the bell tower of the most famous cathedral in Kiev, St Sophia, which is on the Unesco World Heritage list. We were accompanied by a film crew from the Berlin Biennale, which also passed itself off as a group of tourists. Once we had reached the top, we closed the door from the inside, stretched out chains and hung a heavy padlock on them, to prevent the security service or police entering. We needed time to climb up a metal scaffolding about 5 metres high to access the bells and unfold a banner 7 metres long, black, with a terse vertical inscription saying 'Stop!' But instead of an ordinary letter *t*, our banner had an Orthodox cross. Once we had hung the banner outside, from the tower, we started ringing the tocsin, topless, to warn women about the plot of the Church and the state against them. We had placards, such as 'Kinder, Kirche, Küche', the famous slogan of Nazi Germany,* and we yelled: 'I do not give birth for your enjoyment!'

We were hoping to spend several hours ringing the bells, but in the end our action lasted only a quarter of an hour. The attendants in the church, accompanied by police, managed to smash down the door and break the chains. These attendants, religious fanatics, behaved like madmen. They beat us like the police had never done. One of them actually tried to knock down the scaffolding on which one of our girls was standing as she continued to sound the tocsin, at the risk of breaking her back.

After the protest, the prosecution opened four investigation files against Inna, Sasha, Yana Zhdanova and Masha (Margarita) Avramenko. This was a first because, so far, all our arrests and stays in prison had been merely administrative punishments. On this occasion they used Article 296 of the Ukrainian Criminal Code, which provides for a penalty of up to five years in prison 'for a violation of public order accompanied by extraordinary impertinence or cynicism'. However, a few weeks later, the prosecutor acknowledged that our action didn't include any elements of a criminal offence.

What lay behind this change of mind? The German team that had filmed us projected the video of the action on a giant screen at the Kunstwerk Arts Centre in Berlin, under the heading of artistic actionism. The fact that this 'affair of the bell tower' turned out to be one of the main attractions of the Berlin Biennale may have played a role. In any case, it encouraged us to continue our struggle.

----

* The three duties of women, in Nazi ideology: 'children, church, kitchen'. (*Trans. note.*)

'KILL KIRILL!'

On 27 July 2012, the Russian Patriarch Kirill travelled to Ukraine for a three-day visit. This visit was more political than ecclesiastical. For us, Kirill is a big shot in the Russian Establishment, who during the presidential campaign called on his flock to vote for Putin, and who encourages the Ukrainian government to move towards the Kremlin. He's also one of those who back Putin's Eurasian Union. Three countries in the post-Soviet area, namely, Russia, Belarus and Kazakhstan, have formed a customs union and are building a common economic area. For Putin, this is a first step towards the creation of a Eurasian economic union where a prominent place is given to Ukraine, and Kirill is acting as an intermediary to persuade Yanukovych to join this dictators' club.

In addition to his attempts to expand the sphere of influence of the Russian Orthodox Church in Ukraine,[2] the Moscow Patriarch is poking his nose into our political and social issues. In addition, Kirill played a sinister role in the case of Pussy Riot, not to mention the fact that this former KGB agent made a fortune on importing tax-free tobacco and alcohol under Yeltsin. Our action was intended as a protest against this visit, to support Pussy Riot who had been meted out a travesty of justice (their trial would begin on 30 July), and to denounce this disreputable personality.

Yana Zhdanova, topless, with the inscription 'Kill Kirill!' on her chest and back, in reference to the title of the movie *Kill Bill*, was supposed to throw herself on Kirill upon his arrival at the Borispol Airport. She didn't make it there as his bodyguards, in clerical habits, intercepted her as she screamed the Ukrainian equivalent of *vade retro*,* the formula

---

* Latin: 'get behind', i.e., 'get thee behind me, Satan'. (*Trans. note.*)

for exorcism to cast out Satan. Yana was sentenced to fifteen days in prison, and they blocked our website for a time, accusing us of 'extremism'. This wasn't such an issue. Other independent sites easily helped us out.

After this action, Pussy Riot, who were then in the dock, sent us a message of thanks for attacking the patriarch. Of course, we also suffered an incredible number of very nasty criticisms, including in various Ukrainian media, as many simple-minded people have a blind admiration for Kirill. Sasha says, for example, that her mother takes snapshots of Kirill whenever he appears on television. She has a whole collection of these and thinks that this pious behaviour will be rewarded in the afterlife.

As for us, our position is radical. We think that throughout the history of humankind, all religions, whatever they are, have abased and humiliated women. Feminism and the question of women's freedom end, a priori, where religion begins. It's through religion that men have imposed their domination over women by transforming them, quite openly, into slaves and servants. Women have accepted this status for millennia. Today, we reject it, and we consider that atheism is the only religion worthy of existence. The formula of Karl Marx, 'Religion is the opium of the people', has lost none of its value. If the religious delusion disappeared and people began to believe in their own strength, life could only become better.

LET'S CUT DOWN THE CROSS!

We monitor the media to stay informed about current hot topics. In August 2012, the whole world was talking about the trial of Pussy Riot. The verdict was due to be reached on 17 August. As 'newsmakers', we had to react, especially since everyone expected them to be given a prison sentence.

Anna proposed a very radical action, namely, using a chainsaw to cut down a 7-metre high Catholic cross which had been erected in the centre of Kiev by Polish activists during the Orange Revolution, without any authorization from the city authorities. Anna remembers vividly how the idea of this mission came to her:

> I thought about how we could effectively hit out at the Church. I remembered this cross on a hill overlooking the Maidan. In bygone days, Christians burned the pagan idols. Well, OK, we'll follow their example and burn this item of Christian idolatry, I said to myself. Then I realized it wasn't realistic to burn a huge cross made of solid wood; we'd be arrested before it burnt down. Saw it down instead! That was the answer. I imagined the scene: if you saw on the right side, the cross will fall down on the Maidan. Great!

We discussed the advisability of this action, which we wanted to dedicate to Pussy Riot, because we feared our own protest would be drowned in the flood of news from their trial. But we had a moral obligation to support this feminist group, regardless of the media impact we might or might not have. We wanted to deliberately offend the Orthodox Church for its incitement to hatred of these three young women, vilified and threatened with prison. The Moscow Patriarchate had initiated their persecution and ordered collective prayers to protect the Church from these 'wicked' and 'blasphemous' women.

Once the decision was made, the choice of performing it fell on Inna because she was physically stronger than Oksana or Sasha. The next day, we bought a chainsaw and Inna went to some professional loggers to learn how to use it. For her, this was an unforgettable experience:

I trained with them until midnight, accompanied by journalists, because handling a chainsaw requires not only
strength, but also a certain dexterity. The loggers taught
me the proper technique; first I had to learn to saw a tri-
angle in the trunk on the side where it would fall and then
cut into the other side. There was still one unknown: we
didn't know if there was a metal rod inside the cross, which
would have made sawing impossible. It was a risk worth
taking.

In the morning I arrived at the place of action and I
removed my T-shirt. The girls tied ropes to the cross to
pull it in the right direction, so that it would fall neither
on me nor on the journalists. Despite the training, I was
very afraid I would be unable to cut the cross and would
suffer terrible feelings of shame. I knelt down and I crossed
myself, in reference to Pussy Riot who had made this gesture in the cathedral before the start of their punk prayer
to the Virgin. When I started up the chainsaw, I realized
that the cross was 3 or 4 centimetres wider than the blade
of the chainsaw. This meant that it would need to be sawn
into on both sides and it would therefore take twice as long.
But we were in the heart of Kiev! I made cuts on both sides,
and then I sawed for a long time, though I had the impression it would never fall. But down it fell, eventually, and
it was a beautiful sight. For me, the cross is the symbol of
a millennium of inequality, murder, violence and oppression committed in the name of religion. I did exactly what
had to be done. To the reporters, I restricted myself to a
brief comment: 'No structure, not even one as powerful
as the Church, has the right to infringe on the freedom of
woman.' Then I ran away.

The day before, we'd thoroughly studied the plan. During
this action, Sasha was on the hill opposite, from where she

observed the surroundings and gave instructions on her mobile. That was in the morning, and we'd informed nobody, apart from a few journalists that we all trusted. Since we didn't want the cops noticing a press crush, we'd arranged to meet up with the reporters away from the cross, near a row of bushes, as in a spy novel. Two duty policemen stood at the bottom of the hill but they couldn't see what was happening up above, especially as the cross was partially hidden by trees covered with foliage. As for the sound of the chainsaw, it could be taken for that of a lawnmower. Anyway, the cops discovered our 'misdemeanour' only a few hours later.

Upon her return home, Inna found herself under surveillance:

From my window in the mezzanine, I saw a dozen men standing there, day and night for three days. When I went to buy bread or meet other activists, they followed me quite openly, taking photos. But they didn't try to stop me. Apparently, the decision to do this hadn't been taken.

On the fourth day, I was awakened by really loud bangs on my door. I looked through the peephole, and I saw six men who were trying to push the door in, hitting it in a synchronized movement with their shoulders. What would they do if they got into my place? Beat me? Rape me? They could have arrested me when I went out, I wasn't hiding.

I decided to run away. I took my phone and my passport and I sent a text message saying 'I'm going to jump from the balcony, come and get me.' I knew the Femen girls were prepared for any eventuality. So I jumped off the balcony, which was 2 metres above the ground, without getting too badly hurt. A car picked me up, and our friends took me to Korosten, a town a few dozen kilometres from Kiev where international trains stop. In Korosten, we bought a ticket to

Warsaw. I realized it would be a while before I was back in Ukraine.

The guys who'd tried to break my door down had followed us, still without trying to arrest us. It's difficult to say what their plan was. Did they want to force me to leave the country to avoid a scandalous trial, like the Pussy Riot one? I have no answer to this question. In any case, they started an investigation, and President Yanukovych publicly requested that the activists who sawed down the cross in the centre of Kiev should be found and punished. So the government had to do what was necessary to prevent me from returning to Ukraine.

After this action, we not only suffered the wrath of the Ukrainian Establishment, but also – and especially! – that of the Russian Establishment. To make things more serious, it was said in particular that we had sawn down the cross put up as a memorial to the victims of Stalinist repression. This is false. On this site there is indeed a monument to the victims of Stalinism, but it's a small monument in stone, and the cross in question has nothing to do with it.

In the Russian media, a huge campaign against both Pussy Riot and Femen was conducted. It's difficult to counter this flood of lies and accusations of Satanism. A real war of disinformation was launched against us, and that's why we now refuse to work with the Russian media. You never know what context our words will be put in and how they'll twist them.

What is certain is that we wanted to hurt believers, to make them realize the cruelty of their Church – believers who, encouraged by their priests, proposed to inflict corporal punishment in public on Pussy Riot. They were ready to burn the three women alive! They should rather show pity to human beings, instead of praying before fetishes which are nothing but pieces of wood.

But we must admit that the behaviour of Pussy Riot at their trial disappointed us. We devoted our action to them because we believed they were on the same wavelength as us. We thought their performance was both political and atheist, because if you climb on to an altar to dance and sing, it's because you're not a believer. Cutting down the cross was for us an act of support to these political prisoners, but also an anti-clerical act, the act of militant atheists. However, Pussy Riot stated at their trial that they were believers and attended church and prayed. This is ridiculous! Their attempts to justify themselves destroyed the deep sense of their protest. People must have the courage to take their struggle to the bitter end. The revolution is always made by young people, carefree and fearless. Otherwise, it's not worth starting.

12

FEMEN FRANCE

When Inna found herself in Warsaw, staying at the home of a supporter, she didn't know what she could do or where she could go. As the plan to open the training centre was already starting to take root, Paris was the obvious destination. Upon her arrival, we launched, via Facebook, a call to French women to join our movement. The first day, six girls came; the next day, another ten . . . And they're still coming.

On 18 September 2012, we celebrated the official opening of the centre. We did a 'Naked Walk', from the Château-Rouge metro station to the Lavoir Moderne Parisien at 35 rue Léon. Twenty-seven people took part, including Safia Lebdi, and Sasha and Oksana, who came from Kiev for the ceremony. As usual, we were topless, with crowns of flowers on our heads. The markings on our bodies and the placards said: 'Secularism, freedom', 'Sextremism', 'Muslim women, get undressed!', 'I'm a woman and not an object!' We joyously chanted, 'Nudity! Freedom!' under the astonished eyes of the people of this poor, ethnically very diverse neighbourhood.

At the official opening of the centre, we had already registered an association, Femen France. We entrusted the management of the French centre, located in the premises of the Lavoir Moderne Parisien, to Inna. Here, she was soon faced with new challenges:

At our office in Kiev, there were five people working from morning to night, and even overnight if necessary. Here, it's different. There's an influx of volunteers, but it takes time to train them. Few are willing to devote all their time to our cause. However, there are girls who could potentially team up with me. Eloise, for example, who's one of the most energetic French activists.

However, I don't want this team to be like our Ukrainian group. In Ukraine, we were a real 'gang of four' – those hooligan women who had difficulty recruiting radical partisans from among the Ukrainians. On the contrary, here we have no lack of volunteers, especially as we're pampered by the media. But how can we work with our recruits? The problem is not only language because, after all, I can get by fine in English. I discovered a different mentality here, and I try to understand how to explain what we do and why, both to activists and the media. What is certain is that I'd like us to keep our 'Femen Made in Ukraine' identity, our kicking and fighting spirit.

Here's one small example. During our training sessions, I ask the girls to scream. I ask each of them, in turn, to hold a placard above her head and shout out a slogan looking the others straight in the eye. Few of them manage the first time. Most are unable to scream; they snigger or look away. This means that they are not sure of what they're doing; they don't have the charge of aggression and hatred for our enemies that we have in Ukraine. For some, it's a game, while we are a radical movement, not in the least funny.

The style of Femen isn't simply a matter of removing your T-shirt and wearing a crown of flowers. Our protest involves attacking our enemy with our chests bared, on his own territory, and being prepared to go to jail if necessary. Most of our French activists don't intend to go that far. They work, they study in college, they have a family, they often have children. Anyway, for now, they're not yet professional revolutionaries like us. Will I be able to train some of them? I hope so. It's a real challenge.

WHO FUNDS FEMEN?

Since the creation of the movement, we've lived with very limited resources. Today, things haven't changed much. Our money? It comes from Internet sales and donations. For donations, the situation is very variable. After our action against DSK, for example, we received a lot of donations from the French. After our action against Berlusconi, we collected many donations from Italy. When we 'stole votes from Putin', Russian emigrants living in the United States sent us considerable amounts.

As for our trips abroad, we accept invitations provided our travel costs are fully met. These are the occasions on which we carry out our actions. For example, in January 2012, a Bulgarian TV channel invited us for a programme and paid for our travel and accommodation. We took the opportunity to carry out an action against domestic violence in Bulgaria, as such violence isn't viewed as a crime in that country's legislation.

Anyway, we are housed in Paris free of charge, at the Lavoir, which is absolutely invaluable.

In terms of our online store, we try to vary what we can

offer. For some time, we've had 'breastographs'. This is an invention of Oksana's, who suggested selling prints of our breasts on fabric. The technique is simple: we draw our logo on the chest of one of us, with acrylic paint, we make an impression of it, and the 'author' signs it. We sell these 'breastographs' for seventy euros each, and it works. There are weeks where we sell a round dozen. However, the investment is low, since the canvas costs three euros, and the big box of acrylic paints five euros. In addition, the 'work of art' is durable. A Japanese guy recently acquired a 'breastograph' to decorate his bar, but in most cases, we don't know what use people make of them.

There have been persistent rumours that we are simply rolling in money. You only have to visit Inna and Oksana, who live in the Lavoir, without heating in winter, to convince these people otherwise. In fact, we have barely found a way to pay for Inna to have a crown on her tooth that was broken by Catholic extremists.

However, we are sure that with the goodwill of our activists and our fans, we will make progress. From our centre in Paris, we hope to coordinate different groups throughout the world. Napoleonic plans!

A DUTCH REMAKE

For us, cutting down the cross in Kiev was a political, not an artistic, action. However, it generated a real interest in the international arts community. Several art festivals and artists have proposed that we repeat this anti-clerical gesture. Inna, who had already moved to France, received an invitation from the 8th Gogbot Arts Festival in the city of Enschede, in the Netherlands. It's a festival of multimedia art, music and technology, which is aimed at museums but remains accessible to the general public. Local artists crafted three crosses,

and Inna was supposed to cut them down in homage to
Pussy Riot. The action took place on 8 September 2012. For
Inna, it was a great disappointment, from which she learned
an important lesson:

> I agreed to go only so I could take Éloïse with me, as part
> of her apprenticeship. On site, three Dutch women joined
> us. We entered the stage, I made a little speech compar-
> ing crosses to splinters in the body of civilization, and the
> chainsaw to the scalpel used by the surgeon who performs
> an operation to save a patient. Then we cut down the three
> crosses, to applause from the public.
>
> I felt dreadful. When I went to Belarus, I knew I was
> risking my skin and I might never come back. When I cut
> down the cross in the centre of Kiev, it was an act of cour-
> age, but the same gesture in the Netherlands was mere
> entertainment, just a parody. It looked like a show, and
> it didn't suit a radical activist like me. This staging, in a
> friendly atmosphere, in front of people already convinced
> of our cause, destroyed everything we'd created during four
> years of struggle. It was a mistake that I'm never going to
> make again.

FRANCE–UKRAINE, CULTURE SHOCK

Once the French training centre had started running, ten-
sions arose between Safia Lebdi and our 'gang of four'. We
were very grateful to Safia for having helped Inna settle in:
she allowed our association to have a legal existence and
she found this fantastic place, the Lavoir, for us. Despite
our cultural differences, we felt we shared the same goal: to
make women free. Basically, even if Safia is a young French
woman, an atheist who grew up in a Muslim family, and we
are young Ukrainian blondes, viewed as prostitutes, we have

in common the experience of humiliation. The question of the situation of Muslim girls is of course an important struggle for us. Gradually, however, we found that we had differences over what Femen in France should be. While we were in Ukraine, Safia could act as she wished, she spoke to the media on behalf of our association, and so on. But when we settled in Paris in autumn 2012, we realized that we had different visions of what our activities were. We hoped that Safia would be a partner, but disputes broke out, sometimes over trivialities and sometimes over more troublesome things. Safia brought in her own core of activists who were very loyal to her, but our new recruits were not ready to submit to her authority and some even decided to leave Femen. For Safia, these departures didn't count, but for those of us just beginning to make a niche for ourselves in Paris, it was important. Each of the volunteers is precious, we must encourage them, train them kindly, avoid conflicts. In short, it was a very tricky situation for us. Perhaps we weren't much used to complicated relationships. With us Ukrainians, everything is simple. We don't kiss people we don't like. We don't smile at people we hate. Safia was for us a friend and we couldn't imagine that our relations would deteriorate. But we just couldn't agree any more; we had to break up with her and the other French activists in her circle, even if they were the first to support us. Our attempt to graft ourselves on to the Paris scene encountered problems. Such is life.

THE EXCLUSION OF WOMEN, THE IKEA WAY

In autumn 2012, the IKEA brand, known throughout the world, published a catalogue specifically for Saudi Arabia, where they were opening a store. At the request of the Saudis, IKEA revised its catalogue. Thus, all the images of women, and even little girls, just disappeared. Only men remained. With Photoshop, it's easy. It's a real manifesto for patriarchy! In the European catalogue, a photo shows some women sitting at a table, and in the Saudi version you just see a table and empty chairs. There's a photo where a mum, dad and child are brushing their teeth in the bathroom. For the use of the Saudis, there's the father and the child: the mother has disappeared. A world without women!

The publication of this catalogue was announced on Euronews as a short news item, but we opted to carry out an action against IKEA. For what reason? The affair of the catalogue appeared to us a particularly worrying alarm signal, while violence against women in the Muslim world is, alas, a daily occurrence. If Europe, which advocates democracy and gender equality, is ready to trade its values in exchange for petrodollars, what hope is there left for the Muslim women on the planet? So we decided to denounce the way Europe was flirting with the Islamists.

We organized three actions, in Germany, Canada and France. In France, we demonstrated at the Gonesse store, near Paris. Our activists carried messages like 'Rub me out' and 'Invisible Woman'. We piled up furniture and climbed on to it, yelling 'Marianne is angry!' and 'Women are still here!'

Despite the damage we caused, IKEA said they didn't want to bring charges because our protest was legitimate. However, the company didn't withdraw its shameful catalogue. In the name of profit, and under the guise of tolerance for Saudi customs, a major European company has proved capable of pandering to Islamist demands. An ominous sign.

In general, our position on good old European tolerance is radical. We stand for a total separation of Church and state worldwide. But why does the French state, a secular state, retreat when it comes to Islam? Why, in European countries, do we tolerate radical preachers and an Islamist dress code? We protest against *this* tolerance, as it is incompatible with European values.

Saudis beat their women and limit their freedom because *sharia* governs Saudi social life, because Islam is the state religion. So we will take on the dignitaries of Islamist regimes, the sheikhs and kings, by insulting them publicly, by attacking them with our chests bared to make them understand that they cannot continue their medieval existence in our modern world. Of course, for now, we will be forced to limit ourselves to protests in Europe and perhaps in countries like Turkey and Algeria, since we have no possibility of demonstrating in Saudi Arabia or Iran. Our slogans are: 'Saudi Arabia, get undressed!', 'Afghanistan, get undressed!', 'Muslim woman, take off your niqab!' The naked woman is the absolute symbol of disagreement with Islam, a total revolt against submission.

THE BATTLE AGAINST CATHOLIC EXTREMISTS

As libertarians, we are supportive of the struggles of sexual minorities. Every human being, man or woman, should be able to use his or her body freely. We are always ready to support them, but keeping our own form of protest, topless, with our bodies covered with slogans and our crowns of flowers. We decided that, if we were to support an LGBT cause, it would always be a separate action, done our own way, and not a participation in their marches or their parades. We each have our own modus operandi.

An opportunity came up on 18 November 2012, when Catholic fundamentalists protested against François Hollande's Bill on marriage for all, and the granting of permission to LGBT couples to adopt children and gain access to medically assisted reproduction.

We'd already made an action at the Vatican, to protest against the ban on abortion that the Holy See tries to impose in Catholic countries and even in countries where there's a Catholic minority, such as Ukraine. We do not forget, either, that the Vatican has still not acknowledged the crimes of the Inquisition which, over the centuries, condemned thousands of women to the stake. We therefore decided to take to the streets to battle against Catholic fundamentalists and the French extreme right.

Other Catholic protests against marriage for all took place before and after, but we wanted to find ourselves going head to head with those ultra-reactionaries. This was also a baptism of fire for our French activists. On 18 November, at Place Denfert-Rochereau, we confronted this procession of unsavoury characters, a total of some 10,000 people. We were dressed as nuns but in a deliberately provocative style. In fact, under the clothes that we suddenly removed, apart from our headgear, we wore knickers, garters and black stockings with very caustic inscriptions on our chests, such as 'In Gay We Trust' – an ironic paraphrase of the American motto 'In God We Trust' – 'Holy Spirit' and 'Look after your own pussy' and 'Fuck the Church'. There were a dozen of us, and each held in her hands a big white flask with smoke, the 'sperm'. With us was Caroline Fourest, a famous journalist and feminist activist who was preparing a film on Femen and who had been following us for several months.

We knew what these fundamentalists were capable of but we hadn't foreseen such a violent reaction, especially in sight of all these people. The security personnel of the fundamentalist movement Civitas attacked us, lashing out with their boots. While continuing to chant 'In Gay We Trust', we tried to defend ourselves by releasing smoke on our attackers. It didn't work: force was on their side. We then tried to run away but they still continued to beat us. Some of us, including Inna, were violently knocked down. Naked women versus studded boots. A quintessence of patriarchy. They broke one of Inna's teeth, and Oksana was bruised all over, on her face and body. The police were not present. Ironically, they were actually busy containing a group of LGBT activists in a nearby street. They did at least catch up later, arresting five of our attackers. And most importantly, our message was heard and relayed in full by the media.

HOW DO OUR ACTIVISTS TRAIN?

The violence of the Civitas brutes showed us, once again, how necessary training was in the formation of our activists. If women want to join our movement, they must imbibe our ideology and our tactics that we now define as 'sextremism'. Basically, this is what distinguishes us from others. Sextremism is a mix of extremism and the female sex, in the biological sense of the word; we're not talking about sexual practices. One could also define it as a 'peaceful terrorism'. We have no blood on our hands, but we are true radical activists. We do indeed want to terrorize the enemies of women.

So it is the techniques of close confrontation that we study at the Paris centre because it aims to become a training school for our activists from around the world. It's simpler and less expensive than creating branches in other countries. Once our girl 'soldiers' have been trained, they can operate autonomously in their respective countries. We do after all have four years' experience in fighting. In Ukraine, we taught activists not to fear the cops or agents of the security services, and how to behave at the police station and in court.

In our Paris centre, we teach facial expressions, gestures and poses, we teach our activists how to feel uninhibited and scream. All this is very important because we perform with our bodies naked, and we need people to understand that our nudity is not that of a sex object. When we started taking off our T-shirts, some media managed to photograph us with our bare chests, without our placards. That's when we realized the need to wear our slogans on our bodies so that people would see mainly our message, not our tits.

Every Saturday, a seasoned professional provides a free class in self-defence. She teaches us how to fall down without breaking a limb, how to break free if the police grab us by the arm or the leg, how to resist during an arrest. In Ukraine, we were just screaming and kicking out at the police. Now, the little girl hooligans have become soldiers of feminism and it requires discipline and expertise. We intend to take increasingly dangerous actions. In Egypt and Tunisia, for example. In any case, we need to try.

It's Inna who runs the training sessions. Here's what she says about her work:

> What I do is transform a young volunteer into a true Femen activist, and then I feel like a true creator. Transforming someone is a complicated and exciting job, especially when it comes to people who already have their own worldview. Ukrainian women have no idea of feminism or activism in general, while the French women who come to us often have a feminist past. But they don't always understand who we are and start proposing absurd things, such as sociological surveys. However, we are practitioners, and not theorists, although I think that the time has come to develop the theoretical side of our movement. So I try to fire up the newcomers with personal stories and examples from our practice. I relate our actions and I analyse them for the recruits: how we carried out such an action, why we did it, what was the result. This emotional part is sometimes stronger than any intellectual discussion.

13

OUR DREAMS, OUR IDEALS, OUR MEN

By reading us essentially in the first-person plural, the reader may not have realized how different we are in our 'gang of four'. In fact, it's even likely that we'd never have become friends, if it hadn't been for Femen. We each have our character and personality. Our goals and the way each of us interprets and understands our actions may differ. This is why we wanted, at the end of this book, to tell of our dreams and ideals, to speak freely about the relationships that bind us, and last but not least, to talk about our men.

INNA, FOR AN ANTI-CLERICAL FEMINIST MOVEMENT

When I read the news from Iran or Saudi Arabia, when I see pictures of executions of women, my heart misses a beat. Sometimes I imagine myself holding a machine gun instead of a chainsaw, to avenge these women who have been strangled, raped, mutilated, stoned to death. These are not part of the ideology or tactics of Femen, but I feel such fierce hatred against those Islamist misogynists that I give free rein to my fantasies. I might end my days somewhere in Iraq or Iran, butchered by a fanatical mob. But not in the immediate future, that's for sure.

What matters for the moment is the movement's future. The Paris centre will gradually take over responsibility for the development of our overall line and coordination of all our sections throughout the world. Each group will carry out actions to respond to local situations, but the main impetus will come from Paris. Why Paris? Simply because it's a free city, where a great number of media are concentrated. I hope to be able to take on this hard work, with the assistance of Oksana, who's moved here.

I think it's time for us to stop scattering in all directions, and instead to focus on one great theme. For my part, this would be, first and foremost, the anti-clerical combat, because all religions restrict the freedom of women. This fight will be our best contribution to the practice of feminism. We'll see if I succeed. We still haven't reached any decision as to the merits of our future plans. Things have gone so fast!

I've got a boyfriend right now. A month ago, I had nobody. Two months ago, I had a different boyfriend. I honestly don't feel the need to have a man by my side. My current boyfriend is an interesting, intelligent guy, and I really like him, but is he crucial to my life? I'm only half joking when I say that young women look for men because their existence isn't full enough. Personally, I'm very busy. I've found Femen, it's my passion, and I don't need anything else.

I still hope that the man of my life will come one day because my mother suffers from my solitude. In Ukraine, a young woman who still isn't married at my age, twenty-two, is seen as an old maid. I even introduced a Ukrainian ex of mine to Mom as a potential fiancé. Sometimes, I prefer to lie to my parents so that they won't worry too much about me.

SASHA, THE FEMININE LEGION AGAINST THE 'BIG BAD WOLVES'

At the beginning of the movement, we dreamed of a political party of women. We dreamed that this party would be represented in the Rada and that the law could be changed to ensure gender equality. Unfortunately, we quickly realized that we could only act on the streets, since in Ukraine, parliamentary activity is paralysed by widespread corruption. Furthermore, we note with sadness that Ukrainian women themselves do not demand their emancipation. We might continue to carry out actions there to force them to think and change, but our future lies elsewhere.

Femen is becoming an international movement, and we really don't know where life will take us because we're building something totally new. We try to be flexible and to invent new approaches, to analyse and theorize what we do. I think our idea of a feminine legion isn't completely utopian. Femen-Legionnaires, trained in Paris, will start the feminine revolution across the planet. A huge dream.

I think we should seek to tackle frontally the 'big bad wolves' of this world. I found this out when getting on to a TV set to confront Shufrych, the Ukrainian MP. That was going it! For example, it would be great to perform an action, not on a street in Davos, but in a conference room where all those presidents would be assembled. This requires meticulous intelligence work, and I'd love to take care of it: to recruit journalists, interpreters, housewives who could give us information allowing us to suddenly appear before the 'decision-makers' at the moment of truth, in the presence of media from the whole world.

Anyway, I'll do what the movement asks me to do. We have a rather Soviet temper, in the sense that everything personal has to stay in the margins. This is the only way to make it work. If we want Femen to be at the cutting edge of women's protest, it's our duty to dedicate ourselves entirely to work.

At the beginning of our activities in Ukraine, I was very radical and I thought: I have no need of men or children, full stop. In our group, you have to choose. If you're devoted to activism, marriage is out of the question. A Ukrainian man will tell you ten times that he respects you, but he still won't cook borscht or change the baby's nappies.

I can see now that this is possible in the West. Some of our French activists are married, they have children, they work, so the Ukrainian question, that is, family *or* career, doesn't arise here.

For now, I don't feel ready for family life. I don't see myself as a mother. But I've been in love, and if it works out, I'll eventually change my mind.

OKSANA, THE DREAM OF A COMMUNE

I always dreamed that we'd unite women from the whole world under our flag, and this is what's happening. I'd very much like our local cells to form communes in different countries – places where girls live on a permanent basis, train and help each other, read and discuss. That's how they can become soldiers for the defence of women's freedom. Of course, I'm not talking about armed struggle. Our only weapon is a naked woman with a placard, bearing a powerful message.

But this naked woman comes into confrontation with brutal forces. I do not like pompous words, but I have to set an example if I believe in what I do. On behalf of my personal freedom and on behalf of humanity. It's for this reason that I'm psychologically prepared to go to prison, to be disfigured or killed, even if the idea of being disfigured or being left disabled scares me. I lived through a nightmare in Belarus, I know what I'm talking about.

I hope some of our new activists will be capable of radical action, like us. For now, I'm not fully satisfied with the work of the Paris centre. Inna is an outstanding activist and a good organizer, but the training that is offered every Saturday isn't perhaps serious enough. I've decided to stay here to help her and to radicalize the atmosphere.

I've never wanted to get married or have children. I have no interest in passing on my genes and continuing my lineage. Better for me to fight for an entire generation to have access to a better life. It's a nobler ambition.

On the other hand, my heart is open to love. I have several boyfriends that I love and who love me. I have my beloved Sasha, from Khmelnytskyi, we've been together for eight years. I also have Max, Fedia and, since recently, Kostya. Each of them knows about the others. Maybe they're not mad keen on the situation, but I can't help it. I don't need to possess a person to love them. I feel totally free when I'm in love, without experiencing any unhealthy attachment or jealousy. This is my hippie side.

ANNA, THE IDEOLOGIST

It's often said that I'm the leader of the movement, but I don't like this label. It's true, when we have disagreements and a decision must be made, I'm the one who decides. But I'm more of an ideologist than a leader who takes the others into battle. This status is more suitable to Inna, who is ambitious, strong and hard, a true warlord. Soon, the overall management of Femen will fall to her.

I'm a few years older than the other three girls, and I'm becoming less radical, more cautious. I admire their boldness. Protests and fighting are the lot of young people, while I tend to look after logistics and working with the media. I have a gift for that, but I'll never become a Brezhnev who clings to power until he dies.

The roles are divided between us. Sasha is our pearl, our 'special weapon', our 'icing on the cake', that we send in to attack at the last moment. The visual effect is always splendid. But we can't always use her because she's highly visible and recognizable! Anyway, she has another role, no less important: like Inna, she's recruiting new activists and she's a ringleader.

Oksana has always been a hippie and a romantic, but when she's in action, she focuses and acts with breathtaking precision and audacity. As supple and agile as a monkey, she's not afraid to fight against the cops. If we have to put on an action somewhere, Oksana does stuff worthy of a stuntman. I have some priceless images of her in my head, like when, small and slender as she is, she lunges at a cop with her boot, or when six cops struggle for a good ten minutes to push her into a van. She's our best professional in actions.

I often wonder how all three will develop. I'm sure Inna, *la pasionaria*, will continue to rebel until the day she dies. Will the same be true of Sasha and Oksana?

Sometimes the mood takes them to grab an automatic rifle and fire a hail of bullets at those bastards who oppress women, but they're passionate girls who have good hearts. When you feel compassion for others, you're not able to kill people. Femen will never be a structure that sends its 'soldiers' around the world to shoot tycoons of the sex industry, dictators or religious hierarchs. No goal justifies murder.

Oksana and Inna sometimes think they will end their days in an action against the mullahs, in Iran or Saudi Arabia, but, frankly, I'll do my best to stop them sacrificing themselves in the name of an idea.

For me, our struggle is more important than my private life. That doesn't prevent me from having a man in my life. Of course, he's very understanding, otherwise we wouldn't be together. When I get home at 6 p.m., I don't stop being a feminist. My boyfriend accepts me just as I am, a crazy woman who doesn't care about what happens at home.

But I do not impose any conditions on the other activists. Some will eventually marry, and this is only natural. The organization must be a living thing, and the more women go through this learning experience, the better.

My personal icons? I love Marx and Engels. These thinkers have influenced me decisively and our action draws on their writings. I'm very impressed by the image of Lenin, even if his project to build a communist society in a backward agrarian country went wrong. How much faith must he have had to shake half the world? A little man who rolled his 'r's, raising up millions of people and leading them along with him . . . it's stunning! I have great admiration for Angela Davis, who in my eyes is the very expression of absolute freedom. But above all I admire my friends in Femen. The future is ours.

The ideal of Femen is a woman fighter armed with a laptop, a tablet and a smartphone. She's a healthy woman, well-trained physically, bold, cheerful, creative. We're accused of practising an inverse sexism. This isn't completely false. Our girls have to be sporty to endure difficult trials, and beautiful so they can use their bodies for our noble purpose. In short, Femen embodies the image of a new woman: beautiful, active and totally free. My girlfriends, Inna, Sasha and Oksana, are totally Femen.

ONE YEAR LATER

Afterword by Galia Ackerman

I finished writing this book in January 2013. At the time, the movement was taking root in France and gaining supporters in many other countries throughout the world. In March 2013, on the occasion of the release of the book in Paris to coincide with International Women's Day, on 8 March, a big party was held in the Lavoir Moderne Parisien where the crowd applauded Femen wildly, and the atmosphere was electric. The film *Nos seins, nos armes* (*Our Breasts, Our Weapons*) by Nadia El Fani and Caroline Fourest was shown by the major national TV channel France 2, a few days before, highlighting the significance of the movement founded by four intrepid Ukrainian women.

UNWISE MOVES

Eight months later, the situation appears more mixed and uncertain. The year 2013 was a tumultuous one for Femen. In less than a year, they hit many a nerve with actions that were not always up to those they had carried out in Ukraine, Russia and Belarus. One action that caused a real outcry in France took place on 12 February 2013. Nine Femen activists, almost all of them French recruits to the movement, entered the Cathedral of Notre Dame and made the new bells on exhibition in the nave ring out by hitting them with pieces of wood. This was their way of celebrating the resignation of Pope Benedict XVI. Topless, they showed inscriptions like 'No homophobe' and 'Pope no more'. As usual, their website published a much more explicit statement:

> Music hall protest by Femen France, 'Pope no more'!!! With the bells of Notre Dame, Femen have sounded the death knell of a homophobic Pope. Femen congratulate all progressive human beings on the departure of the fascist Benedict XVI from his position as godfather of the Catholic mafia. Symbolically, this date coincides with the introduction in France of the law on homosexual marriage of which the former Pope was a vehement opponent. Femen welcomes the total capitulation of the Middle Ages and homophobia. Pope, go to hell! Long live reason, long live freedom!

This action even aroused negative reactions among many of Femen's supporters. Their reaction was summed up by the socialist mayor of Paris, Bertrand Delanoë, who condemned 'an act which caricatures the good fight for gender equality and unnecessarily shocks many believers'.

Another very controversial fight has been the one that Femen is conducting against Islamism. The most emblematic action was on 3 April 2013 when three members of Femen burned a black flag with the *shahada* (the testimony of faith in Islam) on it outside the Great Mosque of Paris to protest against the detention in prison of a young Tunisian woman, Amina Sboui, who had joined their group as a long-distance supporter. In their statement, the Femen spoke of 'the auto-da-fé of a Salafi flag' and called for 'a global war, the war of topless *jihad* throughout the world'. They were ready to 'breastfeed revolution' with their breasts, in the name of a 'real Arab Spring'. And they concluded: 'Long live topless *jihad*; tremble, you infidels! Our breasts are deadlier than your stones!'

Again, negative reactions were not long in coming. Six activists of Femen (out of barely a few dozen) left the movement in protest. 'It's weird to choose the Mosque of Paris to target Salafism or Tunisia, but never mind. The Femen aren't always very subtle,' quipped one influential left-wing website, Rue 89. And wham! – having just emerged from prison and arrived in France, Amina left Femen in August 2013, saying, 'I do not want my name to be associated with an Islamophobic organization.' This was despite the fact that three French Femen, Joséphine, Marguerite and Pauline, were sentenced to four months in prison in Tunisia for defending Amina and women's freedom in that country.

If Femen are subjected to such reactions from people who generally share their ideas, it's because they don't go in for a ladylike approach. Living in Ukraine in a brutal post-communist world, they were not very well prepared when it came to diving into a complex, subtle, generally tolerant and multicultural Western society. Of course, the issues are essentially the same here in the West: women have still not attained complete equality with men, all three monotheistic religions are by definition the bearers of conservative values and are against gay marriage and abortion, machismo has not been totally defeated, and prostitution is thriving, fuelled in part by recruits from Eastern Europe, etc. Yet Western society is far more advanced on these questions than are Ukraine and Russia.

But these young women arrived in France without knowing

a word of French and with only basic English, and decided to
swing into action straightaway, without actually being given
any advice (or perhaps being given bad advice). How else are
we to explain their misunderstanding of the Catholic Church?
The Church in France is separated from the state; it is simply
a major association for worship, and therefore has no influence on political affairs. The Church of France, just like the
Vatican, has spoken out strongly against gay marriage, true:
but that did not stop the National Assembly passing the law
called 'marriage for all'. So why aim nonsensical insults at this
Church and its spiritual leader, the Pope?

The mistake is just as grave when it comes to Islam.
Describing Muslims as 'infidels' and burning their flag (even
if it is used by Salafis, who are indeed diehard fundamentalists) is a gesture that does a disservice to the cause of
women and civil liberties in the Arab and Muslim world. Is
it any wonder that the good intentions of the Femen, who
are sincerely sympathetic to the plight of oppressed Muslim
women, should provoke negative reactions from these very
same women, who detect a whiff of imperialism in the attitude of the Femen? The most telling example is the cartoon
by a young Egyptian woman, Deena Mohamed, whose
super-heroine Qahera, a woman in a hijab, fights both sexual
harassment, misogyny and Islamophobia. In one episode,
she flattens the Femen who have come to liberate Muslim
women, saying: 'You seem unable to understand that we do
not need your help.'

This lack of understanding of how complex the realities
of Western society may be, and French society in particular,
even though the centre of the movement is now in France,
is also reflected in one of Femen's recent actions. On 26
October 2013, a group of activists took the leader of the
National Front, Marine Le Pen, by surprise as she was visiting Fougères, a small town in Brittany. The topless Femen

'held out their hands to her, to oppose fascist ideas'. They used their tweets to address Marine Le Pen: 'Stop xenophobia, homophobia and hatred', 'Don't try to change the people of France, simply try to make yourself one of them. You can change, it's never too late!'

Apparently, Femen were ill-advised. How else can we explain their willingness to reach out to the woman who embodies everything they are fighting? The Pope is accused of being a fascist, while Marine Le Pen, whose xenophobia is her stock in trade, might still be 'salvaged'? This move only provoked a scathing response from Marine Le Pen, the face of the extreme right, who is known (like her father) for the art of repartee. The woman who makes the fight against immigration her hobbyhorse simply replied: 'Now they're even importing political dissidents from Ukraine!'

UKRAINE IS OVER

While throwing themselves into their 'European' campaigns, the Femen have not forgotten their traditional enemies. On 8 April 2013, in Hanover, five activists including two Ukrainians, Oksana and Sasha, launched an assault on Russian President Vladimir Putin, who was visiting an industrial exhibition, with Angela Merkel, the German Chancellor. On their bare torsos, they wrote extreme slogans like 'F… dictator!' In their blog, they called on 150 million Russians to scream at the tops of their voices the slogan that could be translated into English as 'F… off, dictator!'

At the time, Putin, known for his vindictiveness, reacted with a sort of bonhomie. While remarking that 'it was better to discuss politics with your clothes on', he said that the girls had not unduly bothered him. 'As for the young women, I didn't have time to eat my breakfast,' he explained during a press conference in Amsterdam the next day. 'If they'd shown

me some sausage or bacon, that would have been really nice
– unlike their charms.' He refrained from commenting on
Femen's message.

The attacks fell on the founder members still in Ukraine,
namely, Sasha, Oksana and Anna, a few months later. But not
only on them. The first victim of a violent attack was a man
who had hitherto remained in the shadows, Viktor Sviatski.
In my book, the four Femen mention Viktor repeatedly. For
three of them, who came from Khmelnytsky, he was their
Marxist mentor, and also participated with them in the creation of the Centre for Youth Perspectives. He also moved to
Kiev while remaining their close friend, Anna's in particular:
for several years he faithfully accompanied Femen in their
quest for ideas, never pushing himself into the foreground.

On 25 July 2013, Viktor was severely beaten by unknown
assailants in Kiev, in the street. He was literally disfigured:
several teeth and his lower jaw were broken. He lost a lot
of blood. Police who arrived at the scene described it as 'the
work of professionals'. The beating up of Viktor, who was
hospitalized with a head injury and multiple fractures, took
place two days before the celebrations, in Kiev, of a slightly
ridiculous anniversary – 1,025 years since the Baptism of
Russia, in the presence of Vladimir Putin and the Patriarch
Kirill. The Femen assume that this atrocity was probably
perpetrated by members of the secret services, Russian and
Ukrainian, and was meant to warn them: don't try to spoil
the party.

A series of attacks ensued. On the day of festivities, 27
July 2013, it was the turn of Anna Hutsol. In the morning,
a man lunged at her in a cafe in Kiev and hit her several
times on the face, in front of customers and staff. Having
grabbed her notebook computer, he quietly left. On the
Femen website, we can see that Anna's face got off no more
lightly than Viktor's.

However, the movement was intent on carrying out an action on the 'the Sabbath of gangers', namely, the celebration of the Baptism of Kievan Rus. But that same 27 July, Oksana, Sasha and Jana Zhdanivs, together with photographer Dimitri Kostioukov, were beaten up by unknown men at the entrance of their apartment, as the small group was about to leave for the place where they were going to perform. After the beating, all four were bundled away into unmarked police vehicles waiting nearby, by policemen who suddenly appeared on the scene. Injured and traumatized, the four were brought to the station where they were held for twenty-four hours. Naturally, their intended action never took place.

Three weeks later, apparently 'unknown' men fired off new salvos in the battle. On 17 August 2013, in Odessa, Anna, Sasha and Viktor were attacked. A group of 'hooligans' intercepted them at the exit of a building at around 9 p.m. This new beating followed the same pattern as the previous ones: the activists had been followed and attacked at an opportune time. Once the attackers had finished roughing up their victims, they left in a car with a driver, waiting nearby.

What was the purpose of the attack in Odessa? Sasha thinks that the Ukrainian secret service, in full cooperation with their Russian colleagues, had decided to force Femen to emigrate. In fact, Anna and Sasha did start to think about their future and told reporters: 'We cannot stay here waiting for yet another attack that would result in a murder.' They also wrote to the Ukrainian Interior Minister Vitaly Zakharchenko, asking for round-the-clock protection. In vain.

As seasoned combatants, the Femen did not however surrender immediately. It was another event that finally forced them to close their offices in Kiev and hurriedly leave Ukraine.

On 27 August, a few Femen activists returned to their

office in Kiev, for the first time since the attack in Odessa. But no sooner had they gone inside than police and explosives experts arrived, following a 'bomb alert'. The police sent the young women outside while they inspected the premises, without witnesses. Is it any wonder that the police immediately 'discovered' a grenade, a pistol and cartridges?

Like the year before, in the case of Inna, the authorities did not want a Pussy Riot-style trial that would have turned the activists into heroic figures, but with this charade and the beatings that had preceded it, they put enough pressure on the Femen to force them to leave. At the time of writing, Anna and Viktor are in Switzerland, where they are seeking political asylum, while Sasha, Oksana and Jana are doing the same in France.

NEW SETBACKS

The departure of Femen almost coincided with the presentation at the Venice Film Festival of the film by a young Australian, Kitty Green, *Ukraine Is Not a Brothel*. Kitty, who speaks Ukrainian and Russian and lived with Femen for fourteen months shooting this film, here makes a major 'revelation'. Behind the Femen, it seems Viktor Sviatski has been there right from the start, lurking in the shadows like a grey eminence pulling all the strings, like some macho man who enjoyed making his puppets dance to satisfy both his sexual impulses and his destructive Marxist impulses.

Kitty Green's film took Femen by surprise. They had seen Kitty as a friend and accomplice, and she'd stabbed them in the back. Anyone with any experience working in cinema knows how easy it is to take footage of some scene out of its context and 'fix' the story. For some directors, all means are justified to find an original angle and produce a sensation. After all, what was so shocking about Femen having their own communications advisor? Politicians and public figures, industrialists and rock singers always have their spin doctors. So what? It's the public figures that we know, not their advisors. After all, it was not Viktor who acted courageously for years, assaulted by police, putting his life at risk. Except for the two beatings at the end that finally forced him to emigrate.

The film, it must be said, did create a lot of media buzz – which, for me, shows once again how macho our society still is, whether consciously or unconsciously. For many people, including journalists, it is fascinating to learn that, after all, it was not young Ukrainian women who invented and built up the movement, but an older and more experienced man, a guru. Several articles in the international press seemed filled with malicious joy: yes, we have always suspected it as much! The movement is losing its credibility!

Unfortunately, caught by surprise, Inna and Viktor themselves inflicted extra damage on the movement. Inna immediately published in the *Guardian* of 5 September an article entitled 'Femen Let Victor Svyatski Take Over Because We Did Not Know How To Fight It', in which she says, somewhat clumsily, that Viktor had not started the movement, but gradually took it over, proclaiming himself to be the father of the new feminism. 'He is sexism, male domination and oppression against women personified,' insists Inna, stating that she has decided to leave Ukraine for France to get rid of Viktor and build a new Femen. Of course, this is a defence invented ad hoc. It is well known, and I relate it in the book, that Inna came to France after cutting down a large cross in the centre of Kiev, to avoid a trial, and not to flee Viktor. We also know that all the actions of Femen in France, as in other countries, have been coordinated with their centre in Kiev and that Viktor remained close to the movement. Why else would he have been beaten up in July and August 2013, a year after Inna had left?

The defence used by Viktor himself was equally fanciful. In an interview with *Der Spiegel* in September 2013, he said that the close-up of him in the film is a joint invention by Kitty Green and himself: 'Together we planned how we could make her film more interesting. Kitty suggested to me: "Victor, in the film you are the tyrant, and the girls fear you." At the end, the girls would then free themselves from me. That's how it was filmed in the end as well. But I am not as bad as in this plot.' This nonsense, repeated by Viktor to other media, speaks for itself: if he or the Femen had been aware of Kitty's project, they would certainly have stopped her finishing the film.

Sasha and Oksana, whom I saw again recently in Paris, will not budge from the version that appears in this book: Viktor is neither father nor tyrant nor overbearing male, but he actually played a formative role, and he advised them, as he advised other radical groups. After all, he had more experience and intellectual culture. The only difference between him and a classic spin doctor is that he worked for free. We learn in this book that the Femen organization has never been rolling in money. This is still the case today.

The story of the Kitty Green film was not the only stroke of bad luck to be suffered by Femen in 2013. Since Inna's arrival in France, she herself and the Ukrainian Femen visiting Paris, together with some French recruits, such as Polina and Marguerite, had settled in the Lavoir Moderne Parisien, an alternative place that offers its inhabitants only the most basic comfort. Living here is like living in a shed where the temperature is freezing in winter. But the large room on the first floor allowed the Femen to organize training and evening sessions, and this is where French and foreign journalists always came. However, in July 2013, a fire broke out at night when several Femen were peacefully asleep, and ravaged their living quarters. Inna told the press: 'We don't understand why [the fire] happened. The activists were sleeping, it was very sudden, and the fire was very intense. The Femen have many enemies who have been trying to stop us for a long time.' Was it a criminal act committed by opponents of Femen from the French far right? This question has remained unanswered.

Since then, the training has virtually ceased. Inna has managed to find a room at the Cité des Arts, a place of residence for foreign artists. The other girls, Oksana, Sacha, Jana and some French Femen, had to find another shelter. At the time of writing, they have managed to move in with artists from different backgrounds in a squat in Clichy, a nearby Paris suburb. Inna, eventually, would join them. For now, they will continue to maintain a presence in the Lavoir, but its closure seems imminent: the place has been bought by a new owner and will change its function.

In 2013, there were also some defections in the movement as it grew more international. In addition to individual defections, inevitable in a radical movement, there were splits and dissolutions. The most notable failure occurred with a particularly active and combative branch, the one in Brazil. About a year ago, the girls told me of their plan to send Sasha to Brazil for several months to train local Femen led by Sara Winter. In May 2013, they announced in their statement that the Femen movement was breaking off relations with Femen Brazil due to its 'organizational failure and financial abuse'. Now, Brazilian activists no longer have the right to use the name of Femen. While this break was initiated by Kiev, the Belgian Femen group rebelled itself against the dictates of the leadership of the movement after only a few months of operation. As its leader, Margo Fruitier, said, 'We have nothing against the movement's ideology, but rather how this group works internationally. We weren't allowed any say; everything was dictated by a few people in Ukraine. This was not a democracy but an autocracy.'

WHAT FUTURE FOR FEMEN?

Margo Fruitier's reaction is revealing. The Femen called for the creation of an international and even global movement. Theoretically, this could have worked. This is clear from the example of Greenpeace, an NGO that uses radical methods and shock tactics for its environmental battles. But to build a large-scale movement you need charismatic leaders, communications advisors far more experienced than the Marxist Viktor, considerable financial resources and, of course, you must be rooted in the countries where you are active. Of all these conditions, only the first seems to have been met.

Inna certainly has the stamp of a leader. As we see in this book, she has always been able to take centre stage. In France, she is not only the main heroine in the film by Nadia El Fani and Caroline Fourest, but she has, paradoxically, become the new Marianne. Every few years, French artists draw stamps showing this symbol of the French Revolution. The new stamp available in thirteen different colours and prices shows Inna. Its co-author, artist Olivier Ciappa, explained in *Libération*: 'I chose Inna Shevchenko because it seemed obvious to me that the Marianne of the Revolution, besides the fact that she was bare-breasted, would have been a member of Femen.' This choice was quite knowingly endorsed by the President, François Hollande. Moreover, France has granted political asylum to Inna, in record time. This darling of many of a certain left-wing persuasion has also been drawn by the street artist Combo, holding a French flag, on a wall of the Quai de Valmy in Paris. Indeed, her way of demonstrating topless inevitably recalls the famous painting by Delacroix, *Liberty Leading the People*. And in January 2014 Caroline Fourest published a book where she presents Inna as the only true heroine of the movement (*Inna*, Paris: Grasset).

Now two paths are open to Inna: engaging in individual projects that will help to keep her a celebrity or continuing, against all the odds, to lead Femen (or, more exactly, what is left of it). In the near future, we will probably see the four historic founders of Femen take different paths. In any case, Oksana has told me of her plans to focus now on 'revolutionary' artistic projects, and she is forming an international group. She also intends to try to enter the École des Beaux-Arts in Paris.

Is this the end of the movement? In its historical form, probably. For a radical movement, five years is a significant period of time. The four young Ukrainians have performed an almost incredible feat. First, they have made themselves known in their native country, Ukraine, a macho country (like almost all of Eastern Europe), where feminism hardly existed before them. Their amazing demonstrations, relayed by the international press, have helped shed light on sexist practices in this country and have led to an awakening of conscience. The proof is provided by the demonstrations of the last two years, in Kiev, on the occasion of International Women's Day, celebrated on 8 March. The Femen did not participate, and the protests were not topless, but the inspiration behind these demands was clearly 'femenist'. Different feminist and LGBT organizations have called for the advent of the feminist revolution and condemned 'the criminal union between Church and state'. Among the slogans, you could hear 'Down with capitalism!' as often as 'Hands off our bodies!', and even 'The right to orgasm!'

In France and several other European countries, Femen had the merit of 'shaking the rafters' – giving new freshness to a feminism past its sell-by date. They have had admirers and detractors, but overall, they have managed to use the media with unusual efficiency to bring to public attention such serious and unresolved problems as trafficking in human beings, the reactionary role of the Church, the still widely prevalent sexism, and so on. They have pointed to the complacency of Western societies towards radical Islam, which, abruptly or surreptitiously, imposes itself wherever it does not meet resistance, enslaving Muslim women in the process.

Finally, in Muslim countries, Femen have created a much-needed shock. Although the majority of Muslim women do not agree with their methods, some among them have realized the importance of their bodies and the need to make use of their bodies freely, as evidenced by the examples of the Tunisian woman, Amina Sboui, the Egyptian woman, Alia Mahdi, and the Turkish woman, Didem Dinç. And this 'virus' will spread, regardless of the bans imposed by the men with beards.

When I finished writing this book, I orally translated it into Russian for Inna, to have her endorsement. We were at my home, and it was perhaps the winter gloom outside the windows that made her burst into tears when listening to the epilogue. 'People write books like this when it's all over,' she sobbed, 'but I'm only twenty-two and my life is just beginning.' I reassured her as much as I could, saying that what we had written down together was just the start of the movement. She left feeling exhilarated. But in reality, her foreboding proved correct. At the time I am writing this postscript, the movement is clearly losing speed and internal cohesion. However, no matter what happens to these young Ukrainians and their fans throughout the world, there will be a 'before Femen' and an 'after Femen' in the feminism of the twenty-first century. Inna, Sasha, Oksana and Anna have made their entry into history.

Paris, November 2013

NOTES

All notes are by Galia Ackerman.

Chapter 1 Inna, a Quiet Hooligan
1 In actual fact, Yanukovych had served two prison sentences, at the end of the sixties and again in the early seventies, for burglary and for assault and battery.
2 *Ban'ka* in Russian is a diminutive of the word for 'baths'.

Chapter 2 Anna, the Instigator
1 The most famous work by the German socialist, August Bebel (1840–1913).
2 A literary theorist who wrote a great deal on the intellectual aspects of feminism as part of liberal philosophy. She died in 1999, at the age of forty-one.

Chapter 3 Sasha, the Shy One
1 Victory Day in the Second World War, celebrated throughout the post-Soviet world.

Chapter 5 'Ukraine Is Not a Brothel'

1 As in the days of the USSR, heating and hot water in major cities is provided by huge industrial boilers that require periodic maintenance that can take nearly a month.
2 The main avenue in Kiev.
3 The unilateral abolition of visas for nationals of the EU, Canada and the United States dates from 2005.
4 The Ukrainian Parliament.
5 Shuster was a former journalist on Radio Liberty in Moscow: after the Orange Revolution he moved to Kiev where he became one of the most popular Ukrainian presenters.
6 Great nineteenth-century Ukrainian writers.
7 Viktor Pinchuk is a Ukrainian oligarch and philanthropist who created a centre for contemporary art in Kiev, known as PinchukArtCentre, where he mainly exhibits the international avant-garde.
8 Name of a large island on the Dnieper, considered one of the 'Seven Wonders of Ukraine'.
9 Higher education was totally free in the Soviet era.

Chapter 6 No More Nice Quiet Protests

1 The area of eastern Ukraine, including large industrial cities such as Donetsk and Dnipropetrovsk, is much more Russified than the west of the country. Ukraine has about 10 million ethnic Russians, most of whom live in the east of the country, but they are also found in the south, especially in Crimea, and in Kiev.
2 The favourite snack of Ukrainians.
3 In Russian, Medvedev's name literally means 'son of a bear'.
4 Actionism is an art form that appeared in the sixties. In actionism, it's the action that is at a premium, and

the artist is usually the subject or object of the work. It often involves demonstrations of an extreme nature (art-extremism).

5 Famous art group from St Petersburg, specializing in openly political actionism.

Chapter 7 *Femen Goes All Out*

1 In Russian, *jopa*.

2 Tymoshenko was accused of exceeding her powers by signing a gas deal with Russia in January 2009. According to the charges she faced, this agreement, contrary to Ukrainian interests, cost the national gas corporation, Naftogaz, $189 million. Yulia Tymoshenko was sentenced to seven years in prison, with a subsequent ban on her exercising any public responsibility for three years. In addition, the verdict obliged her to pay this sum back to Naftogaz. According to the EU and the United States, this was a political trial aimed at neutralizing the most emblematic figure in the opposition.

3 Acronym for 'universal central store'.

4 That is, *ts* (one letter in Ukrainian and Russian).

5 Artificial famine organized by Stalin, in 1932–3, to force the Ukrainians to accept collectivization. According to different assessments, it resulted in the deaths of between 4 and 7 million Ukrainians. Yushchenko demanded that the UN should recognize the famine as genocide, but his appeal was not heard.

6 Italian: 'Silvio, what the fuck are you doing?'

7 Title of a German medieval treatise against witchcraft and witches.

8 According to the concurring evaluations of independent observers, fraud affected 15–20 per cent of the votes that were 'stolen' by the ruling party, United Russia.

9 Symbol of the Tsarist Empire.

10 Pussy Riot's action took place on 21 February 2012. They were arrested, tried and sentenced: two of them were given two years in jail, and the third was given a two-year suspended sentence.

11 The opposition in Russia protested in particular against the party in power, United Russia, which they called a 'party of crooks and thieves'.

Chapter 8 In Belarus: A Dramatic Experience

1 Alexander Lukashenko has been president of Belarus since 1994. This country is considered to be the last dictatorship in Europe and is subject to various sanctions on the part of the EU and the United States.

2 So-called 'special purpose' units, used in particular to suppress protesters.

3 In 1999–2000, there were several cases of disappearances of political opponents and other elements deemed to be 'troublemakers' by the regime. According to some reports, these people were abducted and murdered by a 'death squad' on orders from the highest echelons of power.

Chapter 10 'I'm Stealing Putin's Vote!'

1 During this month-long electoral process, between the general election in December 2011 and the presidential election in March 2012, Putin was systematically called a 'rat' and a 'thief' by the Russian opposition.

2 Russian writer, founder of the banned National Bolshevik Party, a radical activist.

3 Racist nickname, widespread in Russia, given to Caucasians and people from Central Asia.

4 Originally, a hetman was a Cossack chief. When Ukraine agreed to become a protectorate of Moscow (1654), this title was given to the governors of Ukraine, recognized

as an autonomous area by Moscow. The status of hetman was finally abolished by Catherine II in 1764.

Chapter 11 Naked Rather Than in a Niqab!

1 Feminist and Green MP for the Île-de-France, and one of the founding members of the association 'Ni putes ni soumises' ('Neither whores nor submissive').

2 A considerable part of the Ukrainian Orthodox Church is subordinate to the Moscow Patriarchate, but there are two other influential Churches: the Autocephalous Ukrainian Orthodox Church and the Greek-Catholic Church (of the Eastern Rite). Essentially, the Patriarchate of Moscow is trying to bring the parishes of the Autocephalous Ukrainian Church under its control.